VEGAN
Foodporn

Bianca Zapatka

100 easy and delicious recipes

lotus
publishing

Chichester, England

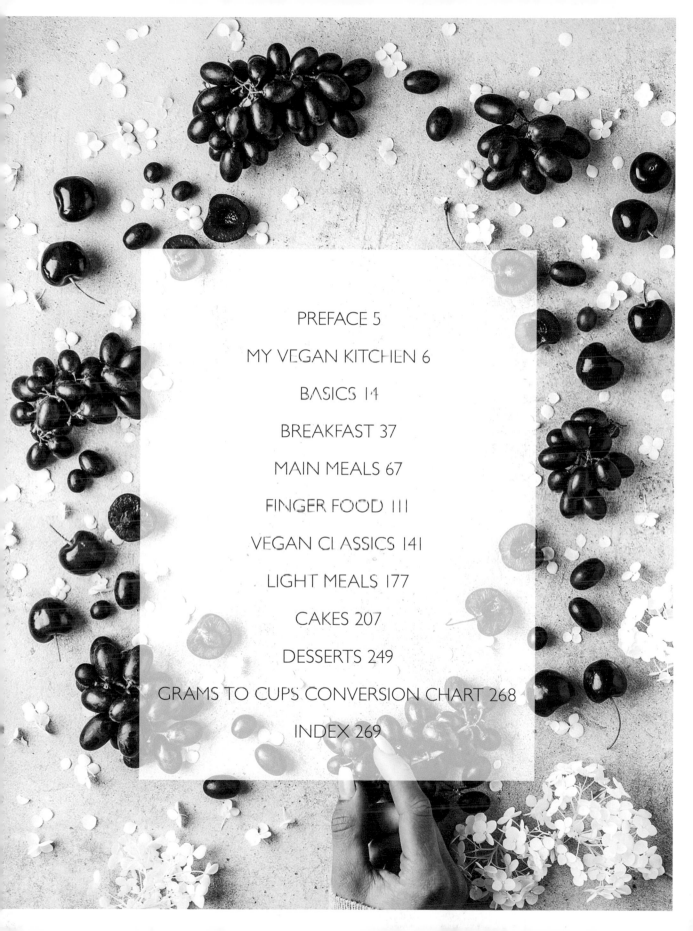

Preface

There are many preconceptions about vegan food. People often think that it's unbalanced, boring, complicated, bland, expensive or just doesn't taste good – none of which is true! Nowadays, being vegan doesn't mean giving up on enjoyment and variety, because pretty much any recipe can be made vegan with a few simple swaps. Plant-based ingredients and alternatives to meat, eggs and dairy are widely available and don't cost the earth.

In this book, I'll not only show you how quick and easy it is to prepare delicious vegan meals, but also how you can use these simple recipes to make incredibly tasty food that feeds your stomach and your soul – and that looks mouth-wateringly good, too! There's one thing I'm really clear about: you don't have to be vegan to try out a vegan recipe every now and then. This book is for everyone who enjoys cooking and good food – not just vegans!

"Wow, that's vegan?!" This is the response I hear time and again when people see photos of my dishes. In this book, I'll show you how you too can wow your guests with your own vegan creations.

Much love,

My vegan kitchen

Replacing eggs for baking and cooking

If you want to cook and bake vegan, it's important to find an egg alternative. Eggs not only act as a very effective binding agent for sauces, set desserts and pancakes, they are also what makes baked items like cakes light and fluffy. That's why it's not advisable to simply leave the eggs out. Instead, there are lots of different options for substituting them. Which egg substitute you go for depends on the dish you're making, as not all options work as well for all recipes.

Flax seeds and chia seeds

Ground flax seeds and chia seeds make a great binding agent and can be used as an egg substitute in cakes, waffles, pancakes, pasta dough, vegan 'meatballs' and lots more besides. To replace 1 egg, whisk 1 tablespoon of ground flax seeds (or chia seeds) with 3 tablespoons of water. Then leave the mixture to soak for about 5 minutes and it's ready to go.

Starch

Starch, such as cornflour or potato starch, is a very versatile ingredient for cooking and baking, because it works as both a binding and a thickening agent. It works for sweet recipes like set desserts or cheesecakes, as well as for savoury recipes such as my potato cakes, or to thicken sauces. To replace 1 egg, combine 2 tablespoons of cornflour or potato starch with 3 tablespoons of water.

Vinegar and bicarbonate of soda

This mixture works particularly well for baking fluffy cakes. As soon as vinegar and bicarbonate of soda are combined, little bubbles start to form (like in sparkling water), which get even bigger during the baking process, resulting in light, airy sponge cakes. And don't worry – you can't taste the vinegar once it's cooked. As a general rule, you use 1 tablespoon of vinegar combined with 1 teaspoon of bicarb to replace 1 egg.

Baking powder
Baking powder is usually used as a raising agent. In some cake recipes calling for just 1 egg, you can often simply leave the egg out and replace with ½–1 teaspoon of baking powder.

Banana, apple, pumpkin or squash purée
Puréed fruit and vegetables help to add moisture to cake batters. Instead of an egg, you can use half a banana or 75 ml (⅓ cup) of apple, pumpkin or squash purée.

Soya products
Soya beans make a good egg substitute because, like eggs, they contain lots of lecithin.
- Soya flour is great for sponge cakes or waffles because it makes a nice soft batter. As a general rule, you use 1 tablespoon of soya flour (full fat) stirred into 2 tablespoons of water to replace 1–2 eggs.
- Silken tofu has a binding effect and works well for mousses and creamy mixtures like cheesecake. You can use approx. 50 g (⅓ cup) of puréed silken tofu to replace 1 egg.
- If you mix soya milk with a little vinegar or lemon juice, it turns into a sort of butter milk.
- Soya yoghurt also makes a good binding agent for batters and makes the cake nice and moist.
- To give bakes like puff pastries or calzone a nice golden brown colour, I like to brush them before baking with a mixture of 1 tablespoon of soya cream and 1 tablespoon oil, plus a pinch of turmeric.

Replacing dairy products

There are lots of plant-based alternatives to milk, including:

- coconut milk
- oat milk
- rice milk
- soya milk
- hazelnut milk
- almond milk
- cashew milk

Soaking the nuts

Why is it even necessary to soak the nuts? Nuts are one of the most important elements of a vegan diet and have specific properties that many people aren't aware of. Lots of recipes suggest leaving the nuts to soak for at least four hours, but preferably overnight. As well as producing a better consistency for mixing, there is also an important health reason for this, in that it prevents the build-up of phytic acid in your body.

Phytic acid isn't an issue for most people, since they eat relatively low quantities of nuts throughout the year. However, if you're going to eat nuts regularly, you must soak them beforehand! Plants produce phytic acid for their own protection. It is concentrated in the seeds or nuts and makes its way into our bodies when we eat them, where it binds to important minerals like zinc and iron, making it difficult for our bodies to absorb them. The acid also impedes the breakdown of proteins. However, it's really easy to neutralise phytic acid simply by soaking nuts before use.

For those with intolerances, nuts can also be replaced with a range of soya-based products (such as soya yoghurt, soya quark or tofu). Some seeds and kernels also work well. If you are going to use seeds instead, it's important to be aware that sunflower seeds, for example, should be covered with hot water and soaked overnight before use, because they're harder than nuts. For softer nuts like cashews, soaking for 3–4 hours is plenty.

However, I would always recommend soaking nuts overnight (for the reasons outlined above). If you don't have time for that, you can simply boil them in a saucepan for 15 minutes. This makes them softer and easier to purée. After soaking or boiling, you should always drain off the soaking liquid and rinse the nuts with fresh water.

Cashews are ideal as a base for creamy sauces or for making an alternative to cream cheese and ricotta. Of course, you are free to choose whatever type of nuts you prefer. You can also use almonds or a mixture of different nuts.

The recipes in the 'Basics' chapter are easy to prepare, and are often used as part of my other recipes.

Plant-based protein sources

The protein deficiency that so many critics of the vegan diet like to mention is actually very easy to avoid with a few key ingredients. The following products are crammed with plant-based proteins and will help you to maintain a good nutritional balance:

- chickpeas
- lentils
- beans
- peas
- soya
- broccoli
- oats
- amaranth
- quinoa
- canihua
- buckwheat
- lupini beans
- hemp seeds
- chia seeds
- spirulina

Fats and oils

Fats and oils are extremely important for your health, because a lack of good fats inhibits many of the body's vital functions. For example, fats are required for the absorption of fat-soluble vitamins A, D, E and K. They are also vital to the functioning of enzymes and hormones, and help reduce fluctuations. However, not all oils are suitable for cooking, especially those rich in omega-3 such as flax seed oil, because when heated too high these oils oxidise and produce harmful substances. It's always advisable to stock a small selection of good, healthy oils in your store cupboard. Make sure that oils are stored in a dark place (such as a cupboard) at room temperature and that they are well sealed, otherwise they will lose their flavour.

The following oils are especially good for dressing vegan dishes:
• avocado oil
• olive oil
• walnut oil
• flax seed oil
• safflower oil

These oils are suitable for cooking with:
• rapeseed oil
• coconut oil
• peanut oil
• walnut oil
• soya oil
• sesame oil

Shopping list: Vegan essentials

Below you'll find a list of products that you should have in stock at all times, because they form the basis for so many vegan recipes. Spices, grains and preserved products last a long time and can be bought in advance. However, ingredients that spoil quickly, like fruit and vegetables, should always be bought fresh. That said, it's always worth keeping a supply of frozen vegetables in the freezer.

Spices:
- salt
- pepper
- ground paprika
- curry powder
- turmeric

Seasoning:
- nutritional yeast flakes
- tomato purée
- mustard
- vegetable stock

Fresh ingredients with a long shelf life:
- garlic
- onions
- carrots
- potatoes
- pumpkin/squash
- cabbage
- stone fruits (e.g. apples)
- soy sauce
- vanilla extract

Fresh ingredients with a short shelf life:
- lettuce
- tomatoes
- cucumbers
- mushrooms
- spinach
- herbs
- bananas
- berries
- lemons
- oranges

- avocados
- peppers
- bread

Preserved foods:
- chickpeas
- beans
- sweetcorn
- tomatoes (passata/chopped)
- coconut milk
- soya milk or other milk alternatives
- maple syrup
- agave syrup
- apple cider vinegar
- coconut oil
- rapeseed oil
- olive oil

Dried goods:
- flour
- sugar
- rice
- quinoa
- dried fruit (e.g. dates or figs)
- flax seeds
- cornflour
- dry yeast
- baking powder
- bicarbonate of soda
- tortilla wraps
- pasta
- pine nuts
- sesame seeds
- nuts (e.g. cashews or almonds)

Frozen goods:
- berries
- vegetables (e.g. peas, spinach or broccoli)
- homemade pizza dough

For the fridge:
- non-dairy yoghurt (e.g. coconut yoghurt)
- soya quark or vegan cream cheese
- vegan cheese
- tofu
- nut butter
- vegan parmesan
- vegan butter

Flour

I usually recommend using a light flour for the best results. So all-purpose flour, light spelt flour or a blend of whole wheat and all-purpose flour would be great. Of course, you could also use a heavier flour, such as oat flour or whole grain flour, but keep in mind that the result won't get as soft and fluffy as when using a lighter flour. Since different flours absorb different amounts of liquid, you may also adjust the liquid if using other flours.

Gluten

All of my recipes can easily be made gluten free. You can buy gluten-free flour mixes which can be used to replace the wheat flour in the exact same quantity, meaning you can make gluten-free versions of my cake recipes or homemade pasta. Thanks to the variety of products available, you can even find gluten-free breadcrumbs, tortilla wraps, pasta, toast and lots more.

Sugar

And the same goes for sugar! You are welcome to substitute the standard white sugar in my recipes for brown or coconut sugar. Other alternatives that work well include agave syrup, maple syrup, date syrup, coconut syrup, xylitol, erythritol and stevia.

Basics

Cashew ricotta

**5 mins + 8 hours soaking time +
2 hours to cool
Makes 2 cups**

250 g (1½ cups) raw cashew nuts
60 ml (½ cup) water
juice of 1 large lemon (or 1 tbsp.
    apple cider vinegar)
1–2 tbsp. nutritional yeast
    (optional to taste)
1 garlic clove
sea salt (to taste)

1. Soak the cashew nuts in a bowl of water for at least 2 hours. (For a quick method, boil the cashew nuts for 10 minutes.)

2. Drain the cashew nuts and place them along with all remaining ingredients into a high speed blender (or food processor), and blend until creamy, stopping to scrape down the sides a few times. Taste and adjust seasonings, adding more salt as needed.

3. Store in an airtight container in the refrigerator for 1–2 hours to thicken the mixture a bit (optional) or use straight away.

4. Store in a refrigerator for up to a week, or freeze for up to 2 months.

Vegan parmesan

20 mins
Makes approx. 130 g (4 oz)

50 g (⅓ cup) cashew nuts
30 g (¼ cup) almonds
40 g (⅓ cup) nutritional
   yeast flakes
1 tsp. salt
1 tsp. lemon juice

1. Add all the ingredients, except the lemon juice, to a high-powered blender and blend until fine.

2. Stir in the lemon juice and then leave to dry out for approx. 10–15 minutes.

3. Spoon the parmesan into a jar, cover with a lid and store in the fridge. It will keep in the fridge for up to 2 weeks.

Vegan mozzarella (firm)

5 mins + 8 hours soaking time +
4 hours to cool
Makes approx. 250 g (9 oz)

60 g (½ cup) cashew nuts
150 ml (⅔ cup) unsweetened
   plant milk (oat, soya or
   almond milk)
2 tbsp. ground psyllium husks
1 tbsp. lemon juice
1 tbsp. nutritional yeast flakes

1. Leave the cashew nuts to soak overnight in plenty of water.

2. Drain off the soaking liquid and add the cashew nuts to a high-powered blender along with the rest of the ingredients. Blend until the mixture is a smooth consistency.

3. To make mozzarella balls, fill a large bowl with ice-cold water. Using a melon baller, scoop little balls of the mixture out of the blender and carefully place in the water. (The mixture is very sticky, so it's best to use a teaspoon or another melon baller, rather than your hands, to help you transfer the mixture.)

4. For mozzarella slices, spoon the mixture into a small dish (or your preferred mould) and leave to set in the fridge for at least 4 hours before slicing.

Vegan mozzarella (for grilling)

10 mins + 8 hours soaking time
Makes approx. 250 g (9 oz)

150 g (1 cup) cashew nuts
250 ml (1 cup) unsweetened
   almond milk
3 tbsp. tapioca starch
2 tbsp. nutritional yeast flakes
1 tsp. lemon juice
½ tsp. salt
½ tsp. garlic powder
¼ tsp. smoked ground paprika

1. Leave the cashew nuts to soak overnight in plenty of water.

2. Drain off the soaking liquid and add the cashew nuts to a high-powered blender along with the rest of the ingredients. Blend until the mixture is a smooth consistency.

3. Transfer the mixture to a small, deep saucepan and simmer over a medium heat for approx. 5 minutes, stirring continuously, until the mixture has a cheesy consistency. Then leave to simmer for 1 more minute.

Nut butter

15 mins + 8 hours soaking time
Makes 250 g (9 oz)

250 g (1⅔ cups) of your
   preferred nuts

1. Leave the nuts to soak overnight in plenty of water.

2. Drain off the soaking liquid and either place the nuts straight into a high-powered blender and blend until creamy (step 4 onwards) or roast the nuts in the oven first to give them a nice toasty flavour.

3. To roast them, spread the nuts out on a baking tray lined with baking paper and bake on the middle shelf of an oven pre-heated to 180°C (160°C fan) [350°F or 325°F fan] for around 10 minutes. Leave to cool.

4. Place the nuts into a high-powered blender and blend using the pulse function. Then continue to blend normally until the mixture is a creamy consistency. Stop the blender a couple of times during the process to scrape the nut mixture from the sides.

5. Spoon the nut butter into a jar, seal tightly and store in the fridge.

Nut milk

10 mins + 8 hours soaking time +
1 hour to cool
Makes ½ litre (½ quart)

300 g (2 cups) of your
   preferred nuts
500 ml (2 cups) lukewarm water
a pinch of sea salt
optional sweetener: 1 tsp. maple
   syrup, agave syrup or brown
   rice syrup or a little stevia

Optional flavourings:
vanilla extract
cocoa powder
ground cinnamon
strawberries
bananas

1. Leave the nuts to soak overnight in plenty of water.

2. Drain off the soaking liquid and add the nuts to a blender along with the lukewarm water and sea salt. Blend for approx. 1 minute until you have a smooth liquid. Then place the milk in the fridge to cool for an hour. This will make it a little creamier.

3. Pass the milk through a fine sieve into a container.

4. Pour the filtered milk back into the blender and mix in any sweetener or flavourings.

5. Transfer the milk to a container with a lid. The milk will keep for three to four days in the fridge. Shake well before use!

Quick nut milk

3 mins
Makes approx. ½ litre (½ quart)

2–3 tbsp. nut butter of your choice
approx. 200 ml (¾ cup)
   tap water
1 date or other sweetener

1. Combine the water, nut butter and sweetener using a stick blender until the mixture has a smooth consistency.

Vegan mayonnaise

10 mins + 8 hours soaking time
Makes approx. 150 g (5½ oz)

100 g (⅔ cup) cashew nuts
1–2 tbsp. sunflower oil
60 ml (¼ cup) water or
  unsweetened plant milk
1 tsp. lemon juice
1 tsp. mustard
1 tsp. white wine vinegar or
  apple cider vinegar
1–2 tsp. maple syrup
½ tsp. salt

1. Leave the nuts to soak overnight in plenty of water.

2. Pour away the soaking liquid, rinse the nuts and leave to drain well.

3. Place the soaked cashew nuts in a blender along with the rest of the ingredients, blend until creamy and then season to taste with salt and pepper.

4. Spoon the mayonnaise into a jar, cover with a lid and store in the fridge or serve immediately.

Pumpkin purée

15 mins
Makes approx. 1 kg (2¼ lbs)

1 small pumpkin or butternut
   squash
olive oil (for roasting)
salt
pepper
nutmeg

TOP TIP:
Hokkaido pumpkin works
particularly well as you don't
have to peel it. You can eat
the skin too. You can divide
the purée into portions and
it freezes really well.

1. Preheat the oven to 200°C (or 180°C fan)
[400°F or 350°F fan].

2. Give the pumpkin/squash a thorough wash and cut off
the ends. Halve it, scoop out the seeds with a spoon and
cut into chunks.

3. Spread the chunks out on a baking tray, drizzle with
olive oil and bake for around 40–50 minutes (depending on
size), until the flesh is soft. (Alternatively, place the chunks
in a microwavable container with a lid and cook for about
2–3 minutes until soft.)

4. Once soft, purée the pumpkin/squash in a blender or using
a stick blender. Season to taste and, if required, add a little
water to loosen.

Homemade pasta

There's nothing quite as satisfying as a bowl of really tasty pasta!
You can make your own pasta using this simple recipe. It's well worth the effort,
as there's no denying how much better this tastes than shop-bought pasta.
Plus, this recipe doesn't even require you to have a pasta maker.

20 mins + 30 mins to rest
Makes 4 portions

150 g (1⅛ cups) all-purpose
  or light spelt flour
  (see also page 13)
150 g (¾ cup) semolina
  (or pasta flour or add more
  all-purpose flour)
½ tsp. salt
150 ml (⅔ cup) water
2 tsp. olive oil

Continued on the
next page ▶

1. Combine the flour, semolina and salt in a mixing bowl. Make a well in the centre and gradually add the water and olive oil. Stir everything with a fork, then turn the mixture out onto a work surface and knead well to form a smooth, soft dough. If the dough is too sticky, add a little more flour. If it's too dry, add more water.

2. Shape the dough into a ball, wrap in cling film and leave to rest in the fridge for 30 minutes.

3. Once the resting time is up, split the ball of dough in two. Place one half onto a lightly floured surface and roll out thinly with a rolling pin.

4. Sprinkle the rolled-out dough with flour and roll it up loosely. Use a sharp knife to slice the roll into strips. Then use your fingers to unfold the strips of pasta and place to one side in little bundles. They will look like little pasta nests.

5. Do the same with the other half of the dough – roll it out, roll it up, slice, unfold and make nests.

6. Bring a large pan of salted water to the boil. Carefully add the pasta and cook for about 3–4 minutes until al dente.

7. Serve with pesto or sauce and enjoy!

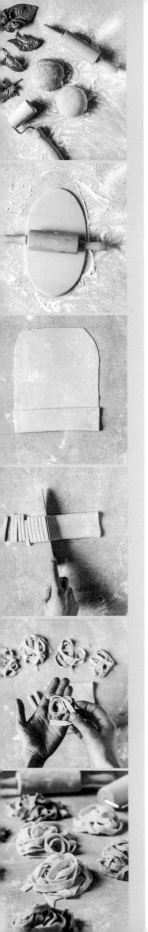

To make spinach pasta (optional):

80 g (2½ cups) fresh spinach

Spinach pasta (optional):

1. Rinse and drain the spinach, and sauté for approx. 1–2 minutes, or until wilted. Squeeze out any excess liquid and transfer to a tall, narrow mixing jug. Add 120 ml (½ cup) water and blend.

2. Substitute this spinach mixture for the water in the first step of the pasta recipe and then proceed with the recipe as described above.

Breakfast

French toast rolls

40 mins
Makes 10

10 slices of white bread
75 g (⅓ cup) brown sugar
1 tsp. cinnamon
50 g (¼ cup) vegan butter

For the filling:
3 small apples
100 ml (½ cup) water
1 tbsp. brown sugar
1 tsp. cornflour
1 tsp. cinnamon
a dash of vanilla extract
a squeeze of lemon

1. Preheat the oven to 180°C (350°F).

2. Peel the apples, remove the cores and chop into small cubes.

3. Whisk together the water, sugar, cornflour, cinnamon, vanilla and lemon juice in a saucepan and bring to the boil, stirring continuously, until the mixture thickens.

4. Add the apples, mix well and place to one side.

5. Cut the crusts off each slice of bread and use a rolling pin to roll them out flat.

6. Spoon 1–2 tbsp. of the filling onto each of the flat slices of bread and roll into a wrap.

7. Mix together the sugar and cinnamon in a shallow dish (or deep plate). Melt the vegan butter and pour into another shallow dish.

8. Dip the rolls first into the melted butter and then roll in the cinnamon sugar.

9. Arrange the rolls on a baking tray lined with baking paper and bake for around 15–20 minutes until crispy and lightly browned.

10. For best results, serve warm right away. If you have an especially sweet tooth, drizzle over a little agave syrup.

TOP TIP:
To reduce the sugar content, replace the sugar with brown erythritol. You can also use coconut sugar or white sugar.

French toast sandwich

10 mins
Makes 2 portions

3 tbsp. chickpea flour
125 ml (½ cup) plant milk
1 tsp. vanilla extract
1 tsp. cinnamon (optional)
1 tbsp. maple syrup
1 tbsp. vegan butter or coconut oil
4–5 slices of white bread

**For the topping
(as preferred):**
vegan cream cheese, coconut
   yoghurt or soya quark
blueberries
blackberries
maple syrup or jam

1. Whisk together the chickpea flour, plant milk, vanilla, cinnamon and maple syrup in a deep mixing bowl.

2. Heat the vegan butter in a large frying pan.

3. Dunk a slice of bread into the milk mixture, making sure each side is well coated. Fry for 2–3 minutes on each side until golden brown. (If you use a large frying pan, you should be able to fry 2–4 slices of bread in one go.)

4. Add your preferred toppings and serve.

Breakfast wraps with vegan egg salad

Vegan egg salad is quick and easy to make, packed full of protein and super tasty! It's made using tofu and makes a great filling for breakfast wraps or spread for sandwiches, bread and toast. Perfect for when you're on the go or need a quick snack.

1 hour
Makes 4 portions

400 g (2 cups) firm tofu
approx. 4 spring onions
100 g (3½ oz) pickled gherkins,
  e.g. cornichons
2 tbsp. pickling liquid,
  e.g. from the gherkins
approx. 100 g (½ cup) vegan
  mayonnaise
2 tsp. mustard
½ tsp. turmeric
1 tbsp. dill
1 tsp. Himalayan black salt
  or other salt
a pinch of black pepper
150 g (1 cup) frozen peas,
  defrosted
fresh cress, to taste

1. Drain the tofu. Then wrap it in kitchen paper, squeeze out any excess moisture and transfer to a bowl. Break into breadcrumbs using your fingers.

2. Wash and finely chop the spring onions and pickled gherkins. Mix well with the tofu, pickling liquid, vegan mayonnaise, mustard, turmeric, dill, salt and pepper.

3. Leave to marinate in the fridge for at least 30 minutes (but preferably overnight) before serving.

4. Stir the peas and cress into the egg salad.

Continued on the next page ▶

For the wraps:

half a red pepper

60 g (½ cup) vegan cheese

1–2 tbsp. plant-based
    cream or milk

4 tortilla wraps
    (20–22 cm/7–9 in.)

2 tsp. olive oil

a pinch of turmeric

To make the wraps:

1. Preheat the oven to 200°C (400°F) and brush a baking tray with a little oil.

2. Wash and finely chop the pepper and grate the cheese. Spoon some of the egg salad, pepper and vegan cheese into the middle of each tortilla.

3. Fold in the outer edges of the tortilla and then roll into a wrap, starting at the bottom. Place each wrap onto the greased baking tray with the folded side facing downwards.

4. Stir together the plant-based cream, oil and turmeric and brush over each wrap. Bake for around 12–15 minutes, until the top is golden brown and crispy.

Savoury spreads

Butter bean dip

5 mins
Makes 1 small jar

1 garlic clove
100 g (½ cup) tinned butter
   beans or cannellini beans
2 tbsp. olive oil
2 tbsp. lemon juice
salt
pepper

1. Peel and crush the garlic.

2. Place all the ingredients into a mixing bowl and blend using a stick blender (you could also use a food processor).

3. Season to taste with salt and pepper.

Chickpea guacamole

5 mins
Makes 1 small jar

1 garlic clove
100 g (½ cup) tinned chickpeas
1 avocado
1 tbsp. lemon juice
salt
pepper
a pinch of cumin

1. Peel and crush the garlic.

2. Halve the avocado, remove the stone and spoon out the flesh.

3. Place all the ingredients into a mixing bowl and blend with a stick blender.

4. Season to taste with salt, pepper and cumin.

Continued on the next page ▶

Quinoa, tomato and red pepper dip

15 mins + 3 hours to freeze
Makes 1 small jar

30 g (¼ cup) quinoa
1 onion
1 garlic clove
100 g (⅔ cup) red pepper
1 tsp. apple cider vinegar
1 tbsp. red pepper paste (ajvar)
   or tomato paste
2 tbsp. cashew butter
agave syrup
salt
pepper
1 tbsp. chopped herbs
a little olive oil for frying

1. Cook the quinoa as specified on the packaging.

2. While the quinoa is cooking, peel and finely chop the onion and garlic. Wash and finely dice the pepper.

3. Heat the oil in a frying pan and fry the onion and pepper for a few minutes. Add the garlic right at the end and fry for about 30 seconds.

4. Combine the quinoa and fried vegetables with the rest of the ingredients in a bowl and season to taste with the herbs, salt and pepper. Blend the mixture using a stick blender.

5. Leave to stand in the fridge for 3 hours (or preferably overnight).

Cashew nut 'cream cheese'

5 mins + 8 hours soaking time
Makes approx. 250 g (9 oz)

200 g (1⅓ cups) cashew nuts or
   blanched almonds
1–2 tbsp. lemon juice
2 tbsp. nutritional yeast flakes
1 small garlic clove
salt
pepper
herbs (optional)
2–4 tbsp. plant-based yoghurt

1. Leave the cashew nuts to soak overnight in plenty of water.

2. Drain off the soaking liquid and rinse the cashews with fresh water. Add the lemon juice, yeast flakes, garlic, salt, pepper and a little plant-based yoghurt and blend until creamy.

Sweet spreads

Raspberry and chia seed jam

40 mins
Makes 1 small jar

200 g (1⅔ cups) raspberries
2 tbsp. agave syrup
2 tbsp. chia seeds

1. Wash the raspberries, place in a saucepan with the agave syrup over a medium heat and bring to the boil. Then simmer over a low heat for approx. 5 minutes.

2. Remove from the heat and break the raspberries apart using a fork.

3. Stir in the chia seeds and soak for 30 minutes.

4. Transfer to a clean jar and seal tightly. The jam will keep in the fridge for about a week.

Vegan chocolate and hazelnut spread

30 mins
Makes 1 jar

250 g (1½ cups) hazelnuts
100 g (⅔ cup) vegan dark
   chocolate, chopped
125 ml (½ cup) coconut milk
   (tinned)
4 tbsp. maple syrup
¼ tsp. salt

1. Preheat the oven to 175°C (350°F).

2. Spread out the hazelnuts on a baking tray lined with baking paper and roast for approx. 10 minutes. (You'll know they're ready when they smell nice and toasty and the skin starts to peel off.)

3. Leave the nuts to cool before placing them in a clean tea towel and rubbing them until all the skins have come off.

4. Blend the nuts for around 5 minutes in a blender to create a fine paste.

5. Melt the chocolate together with the coconut milk, maple syrup and salt in a heat-proof bowl over a pan of boiling water.

6. Add to the nut paste and blend until creamy.

7. Transfer to a clean jar, seal tightly and store in the fridge. The spread will keep for about a week.

Vanilla crêpes with raspberries

15 mins
Makes 2–3 crêpes

125 g (1 cup) spelt flour
1 tsp. vanilla extract
1 portion of your preferred egg
   substitute (see pages 6–7)
160 ml (⅔ cup) plant milk
   of your choice
80 ml (⅓ cup) sparkling water or
   more milk
2–3 tbsp. coconut sugar
coconut oil for frying

For the topping:
coconut yoghurt
raspberries
strawberries
pomegranate seeds
peanut butter

1. Whisk together the flour, vanilla extract, egg substitute, milk, water and sugar.

2. Leave the batter to stand for approx. 5 minutes.

3. For thinner crêpes, add a little more milk. For thicker crêpes, add more flour.

4. Wash the berries and remove any stems. Spread coconut yoghurt onto the crêpes and sprinkle with the pomegranate seeds and berries. Drizzle with peanut butter.

Porridge

10 mins
Makes 1 portion

400 ml (1⅔ cups) plant milk
   of your choice
80 g (1 cup) fine oats
2 tbsp. protein powder,
   e.g. vanilla (optional)
cinnamon
maple syrup

For the topping:
1 banana
50 g (⅓ cup) pomegranate seeds
50 g (⅓ cup) raspberries
1 tsp. peanut butter
20 g (¼ cup) vegan chocolate

1. Peel and slice the banana. Halve the pomegranate and remove the seeds. Wash the raspberries.

2. Bring the milk to the boil in a small saucepan.

3. Add the oats and leave to simmer for a short while, stirring occasionally.

4. If you're using it, mix the protein powder with a little water and stir into the porridge. Season to taste with cinnamon and maple syrup.

5. Add half the fruit.

6. Once it has reached the desired consistency, spoon the porridge into a bowl and garnish with the rest of the fruit, along with the peanut butter and chocolate.

Oat bars

20 mins + 1 hour 15 mins
to cool
Makes 8

265 g (3 cups) fine oats
¼ tsp. salt
120 ml (½ cup) coconut oil
1–2 tbsp. date syrup
  or maple syrup

For the chocolate filling:

140 g (1 cup) vegan dark
  chocolate (70% cocoa)
120 ml (½ cup) sesame
  paste (tahini) or nut
  butter, e.g. peanut or
  almond butter
2 tbsp. date syrup
  or maple syrup

1. Place 110 g (1⅓ cups) of the oats into a food processor and blend into flour. Transfer to a dish. Add the rest of the oats and the salt and give it a good stir.

2. Melt the coconut oil and add this to the oat mixture together with the date syrup. Mix well.

3. Line a square mould (18 × 18 cm [7 × 7 in.]) with baking paper. Add about two-thirds of the oat mixture and press into the mould. Place in the fridge for 15 minutes.

4. While you're waiting for the mixture to cool, prepare the chocolate filling. Break the chocolate up into small pieces and place into a heatproof bowl. Add the tahini and date syrup and melt over a pan of simmering water, stirring occasionally.

5. Pour the chocolate mixture over the first layer of oats and then add the remaining oat mixture. Return to the fridge for 30–60 minutes and then enjoy!

Coconut rice pudding with cherry compote

30 mins
Makes 2 portions

150 ml (⅔ cup) water
1 tin (400 ml/1⅔ cups)
   coconut milk
150 g (¾ cup) pudding rice
a pinch of salt
approx. 3 tbsp. agave syrup
2 tbsp. desiccated coconut

For the cherry compote:
150 g (⅔ cup) cherries
   (from a jar or tin)
125 ml (½ cup) cherry juice
½ tbsp. cornflour
a squeeze of lemon
⅓ tsp. vanilla extract

1. Add the water, coconut milk, rice and a pinch of salt to a saucepan and bring to the boil. Cook over a low heat for around 20–25 minutes, stirring frequently, until the mixture is soft and creamy. Sweeten to taste and stir in the desiccated coconut.

2. While the rice is cooking, make the cherry compote. Whisk 2–3 tbsp. of the cherry juice with the cornflour. Bring the rest of the cherry juice to the boil. Stir in the cherry juice and cornflour mixture and bring to the boil for a second time.

3. Add the cherries and warm through briefly. Season to taste with a squeeze of lemon juice or vanilla extract. You can also add sweetener, if you like.

Vanilla pancakes with blueberry cream and white chocolate

35 mins
Makes 2 portions

1 ripe banana
approx. 90 ml (⅓ cup) plant milk
3 tbsp. mineral water
1 tbsp. nut butter
approx. 2 tbsp. maple syrup
125 g (1 cup) flour
2 tsp. baking powder
a little vanilla extract
cinnamon
coconut oil for frying

For the blueberry cream:
100 g (½ cup) blueberries
1 tin (400 ml/1¾ cups) full-fat
  coconut milk (chilled)
2–3 tbsp. icing sugar
1–2 tsp. vanilla extract
½ tsp. cream of tartar

For the topping:
100 g (½ cup) blueberries
100 g (½ cup) blackberries
50 g (⅓ cup) vegan
  white chocolate

1. Peel the banana, place into a dish and mash with a fork. Stir in the milk, mineral water, maple syrup, nut butter and vanilla extract.

2. In a separate bowl, combine the flour, baking powder and cinnamon and then add to the milk mixture, stirring continuously.

3. Stir well to form a creamy and fairly stiff batter (for thinner pancakes, add a little more milk or, for thicker pancakes, add a little more flour).

4. Leave the batter to stand for approx. 10 minutes.

5. While you're waiting, wash the blueberries, place them in a high-sided container and purée using a stick blender. Remove the coconut milk from the fridge (it needs to left in the fridge for at least 24 hours), open it carefully without shaking the can, and spoon the solidified cream into a mixing bowl.

6. Whisk the coconut cream with a hand mixer until creamy. Add the vanilla extract, icing sugar and cream of tartar and beat for approx. 1–2 minutes. Stir in the puréed blueberries and place the cream in the fridge.

7. Heat the coconut oil in a large frying pan over a medium heat. Spoon approx. 2 tbsp. batter per pancake into the pan. As soon as little bubbles start to form on the top, turn the pancakes over (after approx. 2–3 minutes).

8. Spread a layer of blueberry cream over each pancake and stack them into a little tower. Top with blueberries and blackberries. Melt the white chocolate in a heat-proof bowl over a pan of boiling water and drizzle over the pancake stack.

Granola

40 mins
Makes 5 portions

270 g (3 cups) oats
100 g (⅔ cup) chopped nuts
60 g (⅛ cup) coconut oil
120 ml (½ cup) maple syrup
1 tsp. vanilla extract
2 tbsp. cocoa powder
a pinch of salt
100 g (⅔ cup) vegan chocolate,
   broken into pieces

1. Preheat the oven to 170°C (or 150°C fan) [325°F or 300°F fan].

2. Mix together the oats and nuts in a large bowl. (If you prefer a finer texture, roughly chop the ingredients in a food processor.)

3. Melt the coconut oil in a small saucepan over a medium heat. Stir in the maple syrup and vanilla extract. Add the cocoa powder and salt and mix to form a smooth paste. Add the paste to the oat mixture and combine well.

4. Spread the granola out evenly on a baking tray and bake for approx. 20–25 minutes, mixing and turning halfway through baking.

5. Leave to cool before stirring in the chocolate pieces.

6. Store the granola in an air-tight container in the cupboard and it will keep for up to 3 weeks.

Overnight oats with poppy seeds and raspberries

10 mins + 3 hours to freeze
Makes 1 portion

100 g (1 cup) fine oats
200 ml (¾ cup) plant milk
   of your choice
1 tbsp. poppy seeds
100 g (½ cup) vegan yoghurt
   of your choice
a dash of Bourbon vanilla extract

For the raspberry coulis:
300 g (2⅓ cups) raspberries
2 tbsp. coconut sugar or
   maple syrup
½ tbsp. cornflour
1 tbsp. water

For the topping:
100 g (¾ cup) raspberries
50 g (⅓ cup) pomegranate seeds

1. Place the oats, milk and poppy seeds in a bowl and mix together well. Leave to stand in the fridge for at least 3 hours (or preferably overnight).

2. Mash the berries and heat in a saucepan together with the coconut sugar. Mix the cornflour into the water and add to the pan. Bring to the boil, stirring continuously, and simmer for a short while.

3. Before serving, add the yoghurt and vanilla extract to the oats and stir until creamy.

4. Serve the oats together with the berry coulis, raspberries and pomegranate seeds.

Main meals

Stuffed peppers with tomato rice and vegetables

1½ hours
Makes 4 portions

150 g (¾ cup) rice
400 g (3¼ cups) mushrooms
1 large onion
1 tbsp. olive oil for frying
100 g (½ cup) black beans
75 g (½ cup) sweetcorn, drained
650 ml (2¾ cups) tomato sauce
salt
pepper
4 red peppers
100 g (1¼ cups) vegan cheese, grated
fresh herbs or spring onions

1. Preheat the oven to 180°C (350°F). Cook the rice according to the packet instructions and set aside.

2. Slice the mushrooms. Peel and finely chop the onions. Heat the oil in a frying pan. Fry the onions and mushrooms for about 5–7 minutes, until the mushrooms are well browned.

3. Rinse and drain the beans and sweetcorn. Combine the rice with the mushroom mixture, beans, sweetcorn and tomato sauce. Season with salt and pepper.

4. Halve the peppers lengthways and remove the seeds. Fill the peppers with the rice mixture and place into an ovenproof dish with a little water.

5. Bake the peppers in the preheated oven at 180°C (350°F) for approx. 35 minutes.

6. Sprinkle over the grated cheese and bake for another 5–10 minutes until the cheese is melted.

7. Chop the herbs or slice the spring onions into rings and sprinkle over the peppers. Serve and enjoy!

Linguine with basil and parsley pesto

20 mins
Makes 2 portions

200 g (7 oz) linguine
a small bunch of basil
a small bunch of parsley
4 garlic cloves
120 ml (½ cup) olive oil
100 g (¾ cup) sunflower seeds
sea salt
pepper
a squeeze of lemon

Topping (optional):
vegan mozzarella (recipe on p. 22)
pine nuts
peas (tinned)

1. Follow the instructions on the packet to cook the linguine al dente.

2. Wash and finely chop the basil and parsley leaves. Peel and crush the garlic. Purée the herbs, garlic, oil and sunflower seeds in a blender and season with salt, pepper and lemon juice.

3. Stir the pesto into the linguine and serve. Spoon the rest of the pesto into a jar with a screw lid and store in the fridge.

4. If you like, you can also sprinkle over some vegan mozzarella, peas and pine nuts.

Mexican-style pasta salad

25 mins + 2 hours to stand
Makes 3–4 portions

350 g (3½ cups) pasta
1 tin (400 g/2 cups) black
 beans
1 corn on the cob
250 g (1¼ cups) cherry
 tomatoes
3 spring onions
1 pepper
1 avocado
your preferred fresh herbs

For the dressing:
1 garlic clove
180 g (¾ cup) soya yoghurt
 or vegan mayonnaise
 (recipe on p. 28) for
 a richer dressing
1 tbsp. lime juice, to taste
1 tsp. agave syrup or other
 sweetener
1–2 tbsp. adobo sauce
½ tsp. ground paprika
½ tsp. salt, to taste

**For the topping
(optional):**
125 g (¾ cup) vegan feta

1. Following the packet instructions, cook the pasta in a pan of salted water until al dente. While the pasta is cooking, heat 1 tablespoon of the oil in a frying pan and fry the sweetcorn for 2 minutes on each side. Leave to cool and then cut the corn from the cob.

2. Rinse the black beans well and leave to drain. Wash and halve the tomatoes. Finely chop the spring onions into rings. Wash, halve and deseed the pepper. Halve the avocado, remove the stone and scoop out the flesh. Chop both into small cubes. Wash and chop the fresh herbs.

3. Peel and crush the garlic and mix well with the other dressing ingredients.

4. Once the pasta is cooked, rinse with cold water and drain well.

5. Stir in the dressing and add all the other ingredients. For the best results, leave the pasta salad to stand for 1–2 hours before serving. If you like, you can sprinkle a little crumbled vegan feta over the top.

Sweet potato and chickpea curry

35 mins
Makes 4 portions

1 medium/large sweet potato
1 red onion
2–3 garlic cloves
a small piece of fresh ginger
1 tbsp. coconut oil
2 tbsp. Thai yellow curry paste
    (or curry powder)
1 tin (400 ml/1⅔ cups)
    coconut milk
approx. 150 g (5 cups) fresh
    spinach
1 tin (400 g/2 cups) chickpeas
salt
chilli powder or pepper
fresh lemon or lime juice (optional)
cooked rice or another
    different side

For the topping:
4 tbsp. cashew nuts
1–2 tbsp. sesame seeds

1. Peel and dice the sweet potatoes. Peel the onion and finely chop. Peel the garlic and finely chop together with the ginger. Heat the coconut oil in a frying pan or wok. Fry the onion and sweet potatoes for about 3 minutes, stirring occasionally.

2. Add the garlic, ginger and curry paste and sweat for approx. 1–2 minutes.

3. Add the coconut milk, bring to the boil and then reduce the heat and simmer for around 15 minutes, stirring occasionally.

4. Wash the spinach, rinse the chickpeas and drain well. Add the spinach and chickpeas to the pan and simmer for around 5 minutes, until the spinach is wilted. If the curry is too thick, add a little water. Season with salt, chilli or pepper and add a squeeze of lemon or lime juice, to taste.

5. Sprinkle the curry with cashew nuts and sesame seeds. Serve with rice or another side dish of your choice.

Tortellini with almond ricotta

50 mins
Makes 4 portions

homemade pasta dough
  (recipe on p. 33)

For the almond ricotta filling:

225 g (1½ cups) blanched
  flaked almonds
200 g (1 cup) firm tofu
120 g (½ cup) plant-based,
  unsweetened yoghurt
2 tbsp. lemon juice
2–3 tsp. nutritional yeast
  flakes
1 tsp. sea salt
¼ tsp. garlic powder
approx. 80 ml (⅓ cup)
  water, if required
approx. 1–2 tbsp. chopped
  herbs

1. Cover the almonds with boiling water and soak for at least 30 minutes (or preferably overnight). Then drain off the water.

2. Drain the tofu, wrap in kitchen paper and press hard to remove as much moisture as possible.

3. Place the almonds and tofu, along with all the other ingredients for the filling, into a blender and purée until it has the consistency of ricotta. Stop the blender a few times during the process to scrape the mixture off the sides. If the mixture is too thick, add a little water. (But make sure the mixture isn't too runny!)

4. Divide the refrigerated pasta dough into quarters and work with each piece in turn. First roll out one of the pieces to a thickness of 2 mm (⅛ in.). Using a 4.5/5 cm (2 in.) cutter, cut out discs as close to one another as possible. Roll the leftover dough back into a ball and wrap it up in cling film with the rest of the pieces of dough. Place in the fridge to use later.

5. Place around ⅔ tsp. of the mixture into the centre of each disc.

Continued on the next page ▶

6. Moisten the edge around one side of the disc with a little water. Fold the dry side over the filling onto the moist side and press the edges together to seal. Now fold the left and right corners around your index finger so that they meet in the middle. Moisten the very end of one corner with a little water, lay the other corner over the top and press together.

7. Repeat this process with the remaining discs and then the rest of the pieces of dough. Dust the finished tortellini with a little flour and lay on a floured baking tray.

8. Bring a large pan of salted water to the boil. Slide the tortellini into the water and cook for around 5 minutes until they float to the top.

9. Remove the pasta from the water using a slotted spoon and serve with your preferred sauce or pesto. Alternatively, drain the pasta and transfer to a frying pan with a little vegan butter or oil and fry until golden brown.

Tortilla lasagne

30 mins
Makes 4 portions

2 tsp. olive oil
1 red onion
1 garlic clove
1 red pepper
1 green pepper
1 tsp. cumin
1 tsp. ground paprika
 or chilli powder
1 tin (400 g/2 cups) black
 beans
⅔ tin of sweetcorn
 (190 g/1⅛ cups)
360 ml (1½ cups) tomato
 sauce
⅔ tsp. salt
6 corn tortilla wraps
 (20–22 cm/7–9 in.
 diameter)
80 ml (⅓ cup) vegan
 mayonnaise, aioli or
 sour cream
1 chipotle jalapeño in
 adobo sauce or a little
 chilli sauce
170 g (2 cups) vegan
 cheese, grated
guacamole to serve

1. Preheat the oven to 200°C (400°F) and lightly grease an ovenproof dish (21 × 21 cm [8 × 8 in.]).

2. Peel and finely chop the onion and garlic. Halve the peppers, remove the seeds and dice.

3. Heat the oil in a large frying pan and add the onion, garlic, diced pepper, cumin and paprika. Fry for around 3–5 minutes, stirring occasionally, until the vegetables are well browned and the spices are fragrant. Rinse and drain the beans and sweetcorn, then stir them into the vegetables, season with salt and set aside.

4. Cut the tortillas into strips.

5. Mix the jalapeño or chilli sauce with the vegan mayonnaise.

6. Spread a little tomato sauce onto the base of the dish. Lay half the tortilla strips on top, so that they overlap. Spoon half the vegetables over the top. Add the vegan chilli mayo and half of the remaining tomato sauce on top, smooth out a little and cover with half the cheese. Repeat the whole process to create another layer: Lay over the rest of the tortilla strips, top with the vegetables and the rest of the tomato sauce and sprinkle over the rest of the cheese.

Continued on the next page ▶

7. Cover the dish with foil (or baking paper) and bake for 15 minutes. Then remove the foil and bake for another 5–8 minutes until the lasagne is fully baked and the cheese is beautifully melted.

8. Leave to cool for 3–5 minutes before cutting into portions. Serve with guacamole and fresh herbs.

Avocado pasta

15 mins
Makes 4 portions

400 g (14 oz) spaghetti
30 g (1½ cups) basil
2 ripe avocados
2 garlic cloves
2 tbsp. olive oil
2 tbsp. lemon juice
salt
nutritional yeast flakes,
   as required
plant milk, as required
2–3 tbsp. cashew butter
1 tbsp. pine nuts
50 g (¼ cup) cherry tomatoes

1. Cook the spaghetti according to the packet instructions.

2. While the pasta is cooking, wash the basil, remove the stems and roughly chop.

3. Halve the avocados, remove the stone and spoon out the flesh. Peel and finely chop the garlic.

4. Blend the avocados, basil, garlic, olive oil and lemon juice to create a fine purée. Season with salt and yeast flakes. Add a little plant milk and cashew butter to achieve the desired creaminess.

5. As soon as the pasta is al dente, drain and rinse with cold water.

6. Toast the pine nuts in a dry frying pan until golden brown. Halve the cherry tomatoes.

7. Stir the avocado mixture through the pasta and serve in pasta dishes with the tomatoes and toasted pine nuts.

Tomato risotto

This creamy vegan tomato risotto is quick and easy to make and incredibly tasty!
A perfect plant-based lunch or dinner.

40 mins
Makes 2 portions

1 onion
2 garlic cloves
2 tbsp. vegan butter or olive oil
150 g (¾ cup) risotto rice
80 ml (⅓ cup) vegan white wine
   or vegetable stock
250 ml (1 cup) vegetable stock
250 ml (1 cup) passata
4 sun-dried tomatoes
3 tbsp. coconut milk
salt
pepper
basil
oregano
1 tsp. sugar

For the topping:
cherry tomatoes
vegan parmesan (recipe on p. 20)
   or nutritional yeast flakes

1. Peel and finely dice the onion. Peel and finely chop the garlic.

2. Heat the vegan butter or oil in a large saucepan. Sweat the onions and garlic for around 2–3 minutes, without browning.

3. Add the risotto rice and sweat for another minute, stirring continuously. Pour over the white wine and allow to reduce a little while continuing to stir.

4. Turn the hob down to a medium heat and add a little of the vegetable stock. Leave the risotto to simmer for 12–15 minutes, stirring continuously and gradually adding the vegetable stock and passata. Finely chop the sun-dried tomatoes and add to the pan along with the coconut milk.

5. Once the rice is al dente and the risotto is nice and creamy, season with the herbs, sugar, salt and pepper. Halve the cherry tomatoes and carefully stir them in.

6. Spoon the risotto into dishes and serve sprinkled with vegan parmesan or yeast flakes.

Potato gratin

When you try this potato gratin, you'll be amazed that it doesn't contain any cheese!
A great recipe for a cold winter's day.

1½ hours
Makes 4 portions

1 medium courgette
5 medium potatoes, peeled
1 onion
3 garlic cloves
200 g (7 oz) mushrooms
1 tbsp. olive oil

For the sauce:
140 g (1 cup) cashew nuts
240 ml (1 cup) vegetable stock
240 ml (1 cup) plant milk
½ tsp. salt
pepper
4 tbsp. nutritional yeast flakes

Continued on the
next page ▶

1. Preheat the oven to 180°C (350°F) and lightly grease an ovenproof dish (26 × 18 cm [10 × 8 in.]) with a little oil.

2. Place the cashew nuts into a bowl of water and leave to soak for 20 minutes.

3. Peel the potatoes. Finely slice the courgette and potatoes. (The courgette slices should be a little thicker than the potato.) The easiest way to do this is using a mandoline. Peel and finely chop the onion and garlic. Slice the mushrooms.

4. Heat the oil in a large frying pan and fry the onions and mushrooms for around 4–5 minutes until they are lightly browned. Add the garlic and fry for another minute, stirring continuously. Place to one side.

5. Rinse and drain the cashew nuts. Place the cashews in a blender together with the vegetable stock, plant milk, salt, pepper and yeast flakes and blend for a few minutes until smooth and creamy.

6. Heat the cashew nut sauce in a saucepan.

7. Take half the sliced potatoes and courgettes and place in alternate layers in the ovenproof dish. Cover evenly with half the cashew nut sauce and spread some of the mushroom mixture on top. Then top with the rest of the potatoes, courgettes, mushroom mixture and sauce. For the best results, give it a good stir so that everything is covered with the sauce.

For the topping:
4 tbsp. vegan cheese
chives, chopped
pine nuts

8. Bake the potato gratin for 50 minutes, until the potatoes are cooked through. If the top starts to get too dark while baking, you can cover the gratin with a piece of foil or baking paper. The baking time can vary depending on the thickness of the potato slices.

9. If you like, remove the gratin from the oven just before it's finished baking and sprinkle over a little vegan cheese. Then return it to the oven for 5 minutes or until the cheese has melted.

10. Serve the gratin garnished with chives, pine nuts or any other toppings you like.

Fried sweet potato gnocchi

Three main ingredients are all you need to make this delicious gnocchi.
It tastes amazing fried until crispy and served with oven-roasted tomatoes.

1 hour
Makes 4 portions

1 medium/large sweet potato
2–3 tbsp. nutritional yeast flakes
½ tsp. salt
170 g (1⅓ cups) flour plus
    a little extra for dusting
2 tbsp. vegan butter for frying

For the roasted tomatoes:
3–4 garlic cloves
250 g (1¼ cups) cherry tomatoes
1–2 tbsp. olive oil
salt
pepper

Continued on the
next page ▶

1. Using a fork, prick the sweet potato in several places and cook in the microwave for approx. 7–10 minutes until soft. (Alternatively, you can bake in the oven for approx. 50–60 minutes.)

2. Peel the sweet potato, transfer to a dish and mash.

3. Mix in the yeast flakes and salt. Add the flour and knead into a dough. Only knead until everything is combined, otherwise the dough will be too sticky. If the dough is too wet, add a little more flour, but not too much as you want the gnocchi to be nice and soft.

4. Transfer the dough to a floured work surface, shape into a loaf and split into quarters.

5. Roll each quarter out into long finger-width rolls and cut into 2 cm (1 in.) pieces.

6. To make the classic groove pattern on the gnocchi, place the gnocchi on the tip of a fork and gently roll it over the fork using your thumb.

7. Bring a large pan of salted water to the boil, slide the gnocchi into the pan and cook until they float to the surface (approx. 2–3 minutes). Drain the gnocchi and, if needed, drizzle with a little olive oil to stop them from sticking together.

For the topping:
4 tbsp. pine nuts
fresh herbs of your choice,
   chopped
vegan parmesan
   (recipe on p. 20)

8. Preheat the oven to 200°C (400°F). Peel and finely chop the garlic. Halve the tomatoes and transfer to a baking tray along with the garlic. Drizzle with olive oil, sprinkle over a little salt and pepper and mix everything together. Spread the tomatoes out and roast in the preheated oven at 200°C (400°F) for 15–20 minutes.

9. Toast the pine nuts in a small dry frying pan. Set aside.

10. Heat the butter over a medium heat in a large frying pan until it starts to sizzle. Add the gnocchi and fry until golden and crispy. Season with salt and pepper.

11. Serve the gnocchi with the roasted tomatoes. Sprinkle over pine nuts, vegan parmesan or your chosen herbs.

Pasta Napolitana

20 mins
Makes 4 portions

500 g (17½ oz) of your
   preferred pasta
1 onion
4 garlic cloves
1–2 tbsp. olive oil
500 g (2¼ cups) passata
1 tbsp. tomato purée
1 tbsp. chopped sun-dried
   tomatoes
1 tbsp. Italian herbs
sea salt
pepper
a little sugar

For the topping:
roasted tomatoes (recipe on p. 91)
vegan cream cheese
pine nuts
a few basil leaves

1. Following the packet instructions, cook the pasta in salted water until al dente.

2. While the pasta is cooking, peel and dice the onion. Peel and finely chop the garlic.

3. Heat the oil in a frying pan and fry the onion for approx. 2–3 minutes. Add the garlic and fry for another minute.

4. Reduce the heat. Add the passata, tomato purée and sun-dried tomatoes and simmer for around 10 minutes. Season with the herbs, salt, pepper and sugar.

5. Drain the pasta and combine with the sauce.

6. Serve with a dollop of cream cheese, roasted tomatoes, toasted pine nuts and basil.

Crispy tofu with tahini and peanut sauce

50 mins + 2 hours to marinate
Makes 4 portions

400 g (2 cups) tofu
2 garlic cloves
a small piece of ginger
3 tbsp. soy sauce
a pinch of chilli powder
400 g (2 cups) of your
   preferred rice
1 head of broccoli
3–4 tbsp. sesame seeds
3–4 tbsp. breadcrumbs
3 tbsp. of your preferred oil
2 tbsp. sesame oil
salt and pepper

For the sauce:
1 garlic clove
a small piece of ginger
3 tbsp. sesame paste (tahini)
1 tbsp. peanut butter
1–2 tbsp. soy sauce
1 tbsp. sugar
5 tbsp. water
a squeeze of lemon or lime juice

For the topping:
spring onions
peanuts
sesame seeds

1. Squeeze the moisture out of the tofu. The best way to do this is to wrap the tofu in kitchen paper. Cut the tofu into chunks.

2. Peel and finely chop the garlic and grate the ginger. Mix the soy sauce, garlic, chilli powder and ginger in a bowl, add the tofu and leave to marinate for at least 2 hours (or preferably overnight).

3. Cook the rice in salted water according to the packet instructions.

4. Break the broccoli into florets and cook in a pan of boiling water for approx. 6–8 minutes until al dente. Drain and shake off any excess water, then let it stand.

5. Mix the sesame seeds and breadcrumbs on a plate and roll the marinated tofu in the mixture.

6. Heat your chosen oil in a frying pan and fry the tofu on all sides until crispy and golden.

7. In a separate pan, heat the sesame oil and fry the broccoli over a high heat for approx. 5 minutes. Add the leftover marinade from the tofu while frying. Season with salt and pepper. Carefully scrape the browned crust from the bottom of the pan to create tasty crispy breadcrumbs.

8. For the tahini and peanut sauce, mix together the garlic, ginger, tahini, peanut butter, soy sauce, sugar, water and lemon juice.

9. Finely chop the spring onions into rings. Spoon the rice into bowls and top with the broccoli and breadcrumbs, tofu and sauce. Sprinkle with peanuts, sesame seeds and spring onion to serve.

Chickpea balls with mashed potato and mushroom sauce

This delicious recipe for chickpea balls makes a really
good vegan Christmas dish!

50 mins
Makes 4 portions

1 tbsp. ground flax seeds
1 onion
2 garlic cloves
1 tbsp. olive oil
1 tin (400 g/2 cups) chickpeas
60 g (½ cup) panko breadcrumbs
2 tbsp. soy sauce
1 tbsp. tomato purée
1 tbsp. mustard
salt
pepper
olive oil for brushing and frying

For the mashed potato:
6–7 medium potatoes, peeled
2 tbsp. vegan butter
approx. 240 ml (1 cup) plant milk

Continued on the
next page ▶

1. Preheat the oven to 180°C (350°F).

2. Stir 1 tbsp. flax seeds into 2½ tbsp. hot water. Leave to stand for 5 minutes.

3. Peel and finely chop the onion and garlic.

4. Heat the oil in a frying pan and fry the onions for around 2–3 minutes until they are lightly browned.

5. Place the rest of the ingredients for the chickpea balls into a blender. Blend to a purée, scraping the mixture from the sides of the blender midway through. Continue to blend until well combined.

6. Shape the mixture into 15 small balls (it's easier with wet hands) and lay on a baking tray lined with baking paper. Brush the balls with a little oil and bake for approx. 20–30 minutes at 180°C (350°F) until lightly browned. Turn every 10 minutes.

To make the mashed potato:
1. While the balls are cooking, peel and quarter the potatoes and boil in salted water for approx. 20 minutes. Drain well and return to the pan.

2. Add the butter and mash with a potato masher. Add enough plant milk to achieve the desired consistency and season with salt and pepper.

For the sauce:

3 tbsp. olive oil

250 g (2 cups) mushrooms

1 onion

3 garlic cloves

3 tbsp. flour or 2 tbsp. cornflour

2 tbsp. soy sauce

1 tbsp. mustard

1 tbsp. tomato purée

480 ml (2 cups) vegetable stock

1 tsp. thyme

60 ml (¼ cup) coconut milk

To make the sauce:

1. Cut the mushrooms into slices and the onion into rings. Peel and finely chop the garlic. Heat the oil in a large frying pan over a medium heat. Add the onions and mushrooms and fry for about 5 minutes until browned, stirring occasionally.

2. Add the garlic and fry for another minute.

3. In a small container, combine the flour (or cornflour), soy sauce, mustard, tomato purée and a little of the vegetable stock and whisk to remove any lumps.

4. Add the flour mixture, along with the rest of the vegetable stock, to the pan and bring to the boil, stirring continuously. Reduce the heat and leave to simmer for approx. 5 minutes until the sauce has reached the desired consistency. (The longer the sauce cooks, the thicker it will be.) Season with the thyme, salt and pepper and stir in a little coconut milk.

5. Serve the chickpea balls with the mushroom sauce and mashed potato.

Pad Thai

40 mins
Makes 4 portions

350 g (12 oz) rice noodles
2–3 tbsp. peanut oil + a little extra
3–4 garlic cloves
1 pepper
approx. 4 spring onions
300 g (2½ cups) mushrooms
2 carrots
1 courgette
200 g (1 cup) firm tofu
½ tsp. turmeric
2–3 tbsp. soy sauce
1 tsp. chilli flakes

For the sauce:

60 g (¼ cup) peanut butter
60 ml (¼ cup) coconut milk or
    another plant-based milk
60 ml (¼ cup) soy sauce
1–2 tbsp. agave syrup or sugar
a squeeze of lime juice
water, if required

Continued on the
next page ▶

1. Soak or cook the noodles according to the packet instructions. Drain and set aside. Mix with a little oil so that they don't stick together.

2. Peel and finely chop the garlic. Wash the rest of the vegetables. Dice the pepper and slice the spring onions and mushrooms. Peel the carrots. Using a spiralizer, cut the carrots and courgette into long, thin noodles.

3. Wrap the tofu in kitchen paper and squeeze out the moisture. Cut into cubes and marinate in the turmeric.

4. Heat 1–2 tbsp. oil in a large frying pan or wok. Briefly fry the spring onions and garlic, stirring continuously. Remove from the pan and set aside.

5. Heat another tablespoon of oil in the same pan and fry the tofu on all sides until crispy. Remove from the pan and set aside.

6. Sear the mushrooms for around 3–4 minutes. Return the tofu to the pan, douse with soy sauce and toss so that everything has a nice brown colour.

7. Now add the vegetables and sweat until they are softer but still crunchy.

8. While the vegetables are cooking, melt the peanut butter in another large frying pan. Remove from the hob and stir in the rest of the ingredients for the peanut sauce.

For the topping:
fresh coriander
toasted peanuts, roughly
   chopped
sesame seeds
1 lime, quartered

9. Add the cooked noodles, spring onions, garlic, chilli flakes and peanut sauce to the tofu and vegetables. Mix well and warm through for 2–3 minutes, stirring continuously.

10. Sprinkle the Pad Thai with coriander, peanuts and sesame seeds and serve with the lime wedges.

Fried gnocchi with garlic mushrooms

20 mins
Makes 1 portion

300 g (10½ oz) gnocchi
   (recipe on p. 106)
1 red onion
1 garlic clove
250 g (2 cups) mushrooms
2 tbsp. olive oil
salt
pepper

For the topping:
1 tbsp. pine nuts
basil and parsley pesto
   (recipe on p. 72)
fresh basil
nutritional yeast flakes

1. Make your own gnocchi (recipe on p. 106) or cook shop-bought gnocchi according to the packet instructions.

2. Peel and finely chop the onion and garlic. Clean and slice the mushrooms.

3. Heat the oil in a frying pan and fry the gnocchi on both sides. Add the garlic, onion and mushrooms to the pan and continue to fry until everything is golden brown and crispy. Season with salt and pepper.

4. Toast the pine nuts in a separate dry frying pan until golden brown.

5. Serve the fried gnocchi with pesto, toasted pine nuts, fresh basil and yeast flakes.

Gnocchi vegetable stir-fry

20 mins
Makes 2 portions

3–4 medium potatoes
150 g (1¼ cups) flour plus a little
   extra for dusting
½ tsp. salt
a pinch of ground nutmeg
25 g (¼ cup) potato flour
1 small onion
1 garlic clove
200 g (1⅔ cups) mushrooms
200 g (1⅓ cups) courgette
125 g (⅔ cup) cherry tomatoes
2–3 tbsp. olive oil
1–2 tbsp. soy sauce
salt
pepper
your preferred dried Italian herbs
a few fresh basil leaves
2 tsp. nutritional yeast flakes

1. Boil the potatoes for approx. 20 minutes in salted water.

2. Peel immediately, mash until smooth using a potato masher, and leave to cool.

3. Add the flour, salt and nutmeg and knead. Work in the potato flour, one spoon at a time, until the dough is no longer sticky.

4. Halve the dough and shape into rolls approx. 1.5–2 cm (½–1 in.) thick.

5. Cut the rolls into 1.5–2 cm (½–¾ in.)-wide pieces, shape into little balls and dust with a little flour.

6. Create the classic gnocchi pattern by crimping each ball with a fork.

7. Bring a pan of salted water to the boil and add the gnocchi.

8. As soon as the gnocchi float to the top, remove them with a slotted spoon and allow to drain.

9. Peel and chop the onion and garlic. Clean and slice the mushrooms and courgettes. Wash and halve the tomatoes.

10. Heat 1–2 tbsp. oil in a frying pan and fry the gnocchi for approx. 5 minutes, turning frequently. Remove and keep warm.

11. Heat 1–2 tbsp. oil in the same pan. Fry the garlic, onion, courgette and mushrooms for around 3–4 minutes. Season with the soy sauce, salt, pepper and Italian herbs. Add the tomatoes and fry for another minute. Finally, stir in the fried gnocchi.

12. Serve the gnocchi sprinkled with fresh basil and yeast flakes.

Cauliflower tikka masala

This vegan curry is made using classic Indian spices, packed with protein
from the red lentils and ready in no time!

40 mins
Makes 4 portions

400 g (2 cups) rice
1 onion
3–4 garlic cloves
½ cauliflower (approx.
   750 g/1½ lbs)
1–2 tbsp. olive oil
a piece of fresh ginger
   (approx. 2 cm/1 in.)
75 g (⅓ cup) red lentils
2 tsp. garam masala or
   curry powder
½ tsp. turmeric
¼ tsp. ground cumin
½ tsp. chilli powder
½ tsp. salt
1 tbsp. agave syrup
1 tin (400 g/2 cups) chopped
   tomatoes
approx. 240 ml (1 cup)
   vegetable stock
100 ml (½ cup) coconut milk
120 g (½ cup) soya yoghurt,
   coconut milk or cashew nut
   cream

For the topping:
sesame seeds
toasted cashew nuts
fresh parsley

1. Cook the rice according to the packet instructions.

2. Peel and finely chop the onion and garlic. Wash the
cauliflower and break into small florets. Finely grate the ginger.

3. Heat the oil in a large frying pan. Add the cauliflower
florets and onions and fry for around 3 minutes, until the
cauliflower is lightly browned and the onions are translucent.

4. Add the garlic, ginger, lentils, spices and agave syrup and fry
for another minute, stirring continuously.

5. Add the chopped tomatoes and vegetable stock. Stir well
and cover, then simmer for approx. 10–15 minutes on a low
heat, stirring occasionally, until the cauliflower and lentils are
well cooked.

6. If the sauce is too thick, add a little water. Add the coconut
milk for a creamier sauce. If the sauce is too watery, remove
the lid and allow to reduce for a few more minutes until it has
the desired consistency. Season to taste.

7. Remove the curry from the heat. Cover and leave to stand
for a few more minutes to bring out the flavours.

8. Serve with soya yoghurt and rice. Garnish with sesame
seeds, toasted cashews and fresh parsley.

Finger food

Wedges with guacamole

50 mins
Makes 3 portions

3–4 medium potatoes
2 tbsp. olive oil
1–2 tbsp. roast potato seasoning
1 tsp. garlic powder

For the potato spice mix:
1 tbsp. smoked paprika
2 tsp. garlic powder
pinch of chili powder (optional)
¼ tsp. salt (add more to taste
   after baking)

For the guacamole:
1 garlic clove
1 ripe avocado
1 tsp. lemon juice
salt
pepper

1. Preheat the oven to 200°C (or 180°C fan) [400°F or 350°F fan].

2. Wash and dry the potatoes and chop into quarters (wedges).

3. Place the potato wedges, oil and seasonings in a lidded container, replace the lid and shake well.

4. Place the seasoned wedges on a baking tray lined with baking paper and roast in the oven for around 45 minutes (or until the potatoes are as brown as you'd like).

5. Turn the wedges a few times while roasting.

6. Once the wedges are golden brown and crispy, serve straight away.

To make the guacamole:
Peel and finely chop the garlic. Halve the avocado, remove the stone and blend the flesh together with the garlic and lemon juice. Season with salt and pepper.

Pizza toast with vegan mozzarella

30 mins + 8 hours soaking time
Makes 4

75 g (½ cup) cashew nuts
230 ml (1 cup) unsweetened
   almond milk
3 tbsp. tapioca starch
2 tbsp. nutritional yeast flakes
1 tsp. lemon juice
½ tsp. salt
½ tsp. garlic powder
¼ tsp. smoked ground paprika

For the pizza toast:
4 slices of bread
100 ml (½ cup) passata
salt
pepper
1 tbsp. Italian seasoning
200 g (1 cup) cherry tomatoes
olive oil for drizzling
a few basil leaves

1. Soak the cashew nuts overnight in plenty of water.

2. Preheat the oven to 180°C [350°F] (fan).

3. Drain the cashew nuts and transfer to a blender with the almond milk, tapioca starch, nutritional yeast flakes and lemon juice. Blend to a fine purée. Add the seasoning and spices and mix well.

4. Transfer the cashew mixture to a small, deep saucepan and simmer over a medium heat for approx. 5 minutes, stirring continuously, until the mixture has a cheesy consistency. Leave to simmer for a few more minutes. Remove from the heat and set aside.

5. Lightly toast the bread in the toaster.

6. While you're waiting for the toast, season the passata with salt, pepper and the Italian seasoning and mix through. Slice the cherry tomatoes.

7. Place the slices of toast on a baking tray lined with baking paper and spread with the tomato sauce. Arrange the tomato slices and vegan mozzarella on top of the toast and drizzle with a little olive oil.

8. Grill the pizza toasts in the oven for approx. 10 minutes. Serve garnished with basil.

Spinach tortillas

30 mins + 20 mins (resting
time of the dough)
Makes 6–8

200 g (6 cups) fresh
spinach
60 ml (¼ cup) plant oil
1 tsp. salt
375 g (3 cups) flour
(see also page 13)
1 tsp. baking powder

1. Heat a frying pan over a medium heat. Rinse the spinach and add to the pan while still dripping wet. Sauté for 1–2 minutes until wilted.

2. Transfer the spinach to a blender along with the oil and salt and blend to form a smooth purée.

3. Combine the flour and baking powder in a large bowl.

4. Add the spinach and approx. 60 ml (¼ cup) water. Mix well using your hands and then knead for around 5 minutes to form a smooth dough. If the dough is too sticky, add more flour. If it's too dry, add more water.

5. Shape the dough into a ball, cover with a clean, damp tea towel and leave to chill in the fridge for 15–20 minutes.

6. Once chilled, cut the dough into 6–8 pieces, depending on how large you want the tortillas to be.

7. Shape each piece of dough into a ball, place on a floured work surface and, using a rolling pin, roll out to a large disc approx. 20–22 cm/7–9 in. wide.

8. Heat a non-stick frying pan over a medium heat and fry the tortillas for approx. 1–2 minutes on each side, until little bubbles start to form.

9. Add your favourite fillings.

Filo cigars with spinach and tomato

55 mins
Makes approx. 24

200 ml (¾ cup) plant milk
2 tbsp. olive oil
ready-made filo pastry (360 g)
sesame seeds to garnish

For the spinach filling (makes approx. 17):

1 onion
2 garlic cloves
300 g (10 cups) baby spinach
1 tbsp. olive oil for frying
250 g (1¼ cups) fermented tofu,
   homemade vegan cheese or
   smoked tofu
3 tbsp. pine nuts (optional)
salt
pepper

For the tomato filling (makes approx. 7):

75 g (½ cup) cashew nuts
2 tbsp. sunflower seeds
120 ml (½ cup) passata
1–2 garlic cloves
1–2 tbsp. nutritional yeast flakes
   (optional)
Italian herbs

1. Preheat the oven to 180°C (350°F).

2. Mix the plant milk with the oil.

3. Cut the pastry into triangles using a pizza cutter. Lay a triangle of pastry with the top pointing upwards on a work surface and brush with the milk and oil mixture.

4. Spread about 1–2 tablespoons of one of the two fillings lengthways along the lower, broad side of the triangle, leaving a 2 cm (¾ in.) edge at the bottom and on both sides. Carefully fold the bottom of the sheet over the filling. Fold in the left and right sides and roll the pastry up like a wrap. Lay on a baking sheet and repeat steps 3 and 4 with the rest of the pastry and fillings.

5. Brush the cigars with the milk and oil mixture and sprinkle over a few sesame seeds. Bake in the preheated oven at 180°C (350°F) for around 15 minutes or until the pastry is crispy and golden.

To make the spinach filling:

1. Peel and finely chop the onion and garlic. Wash, drain and sauté the spinach for 1–2 minutes, or until wilted. Heat the oil in a frying pan and fry the onion for 1–2 minutes. Add the garlic and spinach and fry for another 1–2 minutes until the spinach is wilted. Leave the spinach to cool a little and then squeeze out any excess moisture.

Continued on the next page ▶

TOP TIP:

I like to use pre-made filo pastry triangles for this recipe, but you can also buy filo pastry and cut it into triangles using a pizza cutter.

Keep the filo pastry covered with a damp tea towel during preparation. As it is so thin, it has a tendency to dry out and break.

2. Break the tofu into breadcrumbs. Combine the tofu with the spinach mixture and stir in the pine nuts (if using). Season with salt and pepper.

To make the tomato filling:

1. Cover the cashew nuts and sunflower seeds with boiling water and soak for approx. 15 minutes. Drain and rinse.

2. Transfer the nuts and seeds to a blender along with the rest of the ingredients for the tomato filling and blend into a paste. Season with salt and pepper.

Burrito samosas

30 mins
Makes 6

150 g (⅔ cup) Arborio rice
2 tbsp. coconut oil
1 red onion
2 garlic cloves
1 red pepper
1 tsp. smoked ground
    paprika
1 tsp. chilli powder
1 tsp. cumin
salt
pepper
approx. 3 tbsp. salsa
1 tsp. Tabasco
1 tin (400 g/2 cups) black
    beans
150 g (1 cup) sweetcorn
50 g (¾ cup) vegan cheese,
    grated
3 tbsp. flour + 5 tbsp. water
6 large tortilla wraps
    (recipe on p. 119)
almond milk + olive oil
    for brushing

Continued on the
next page ▶

1. Cook the rice according to the packet instructions.

2. Peel and finely chop the onion and garlic. Dice the pepper. Heat the oil in a large frying pan and fry the onion for 1–2 minutes until translucent.

3. Add the garlic and pepper and fry for a little longer to soften the pepper, stirring continuously.

4. Add the paprika, chilli powder, cumin, salt and pepper and briefly sauté.

5. Add the rice, salsa and Tabasco and mix well.

6. Rinse and drain the beans and sweetcorn and stir them in.

7. Leave the rice to cool before mixing in the vegan cheese.

8. Mix the flour and water in a small cup and set aside.

To make the samosas:

1. Cut the tortillas into quarters and fold each quarter to make a pouch. Brush the outer edges with the flour paste and press together.

2. Fill each pouch with approx. 1–2 tbsp. of the rice mixture (but not so much that you won't be able to seal them well). Brush the top edges of the pouch with a little paste and seal.

Cashew dip:

150 g (1 cup) cashew nuts,
   soaked overnight
75 ml (⅓ cup) water
2 tbsp. nutritional yeast
   flakes
1–2 tsp. lemon juice
approx. 1 tsp. salt
¼ tsp. garlic powder
¼ tsp. smoked ground
   paprika

To make the guacamole:

1 ripe avocado
1 garlic clove, chopped
1 tsp. lemon juice

TOP TIP:

You can easily modify this
recipe, for example by
filling the samosas with
the spinach and tomato
mixtures for the filo cigars
(recipe on p. 121).

3. Repeat this process until all the ingredients have
been used up.

4. Mix the almond milk with the oil.

5. Lay the samosas on a baking tray lined with
baking paper, with the folded side facing down.
Brush with a little almond milk and oil.

6. Bake in a preheated oven at 200°C (400°F)
for approx. 15 minutes, until the tops are lightly
browned and crispy. Serve with the dips.

To make the dips:

1. Combine all the ingredients for the cashew dip
and season to taste.

2. To make the guacamole, halve the avocado,
remove the stone and purée the flesh together
with the rest of the ingredients. Season to taste.

Croquettes

A simple recipe for vegan croquettes with spinach. Crispy on the outside and soft and creamy on the inside, they make the perfect evening snack or party dish.

30 mins + 4 hours to freeze
Makes 30

250 g (8 cups) frozen spinach
½ onion
2 garlic cloves
400 ml (1⅔ cups) unsweetened
  plant milk
120 ml (½ cup) vegetable stock
3 tbsp. olive oil or vegan butter
75 g (⅔ cup) flour
½ tsp. salt
pepper

For the breadcrumb coating:
approx. 250 ml (1 cup) plant milk
135 g (1⅛ cups) breadcrumbs
coconut oil for frying

TOP TIP:
The croquettes taste best when they're fresh out of the pan and stay nice and soft even once they've cooled down.

1. Defrost the spinach and squeeze out any excess moisture.

2. Peel and finely chop the onion and garlic.

3. Combine 400 ml (1⅔ cups) plant milk with the vegetable stock in a jug.

4. Heat the olive oil in a large saucepan over a medium heat. Add the onion and fry until soft. Once the onion has softened, add the garlic and continue to sweat for 1–2 minutes.

5. Sieve the flour into the pan, stirring well to prevent it from burning. As soon as the mixture starts to lightly brown, gradually add the milk mixture. Keep stirring until the milk and flour has combined to form a smooth, creamy sauce with no lumps.

6. Add the spinach and season with salt and pepper.

7. Leave the mixture to cool and then chill in the fridge for at least 3–4 hours (preferably overnight).

8. To make the breadcrumb coating, pour approx. 250 ml (1 cup) plant milk into a bowl. Place the breadcrumbs in another bowl. Take approx. 1 teaspoon of the filling and roll into a croquette shape. Roll the croquettes in the breadcrumbs, then dip into the plant milk, then roll in the breadcrumbs again.

9. Heat the coconut oil in a frying pan and fry the croquettes until golden brown. Remove from the pan and place on a plate (or baking tray) lined with kitchen paper to soak up the excess oil.

10. Allow to cool a little before serving.

Spinach empanadas

These little vegan pasties are perfect for buffets and are delicious hot or cold.

30 mins + 30 mins to cool
Makes 4 portions

300 g (2⅓ cups) flour
1 tsp. baking powder
1 tsp. salt
100 g (½ cup) vegan butter
150 ml (⅔ cup) lukewarm
   plant milk

For the filling:
300 g (10 cups) frozen spinach
1 onion
2 garlic cloves
3 tsp. olive oil
150 g (1¾ cups) vegan
   cheese, grated
salt
pepper
nutmeg, to taste
chilli powder, to taste

To brush:
1–2 tbsp. olive oil
3 tbsp. soya milk
a pinch of turmeric

1. Mix the flour, baking powder and salt in a large bowl. Make a well in the centre.

2. Melt the vegan butter in a saucepan, allow to cool slightly and then pour into the well. Pour in the plant milk and knead everything into a nice smooth dough.

3. Shape the dough into a ball, wrap in cling film and place in the fridge to chill for at least 30 minutes.

To make the filling:
1. Defrost the spinach and squeeze out any excess moisture.

2. Peel and finely chop the onion and garlic.

3. Heat the oil in a frying pan. Briefly sauté the garlic and onion. Add the spinach and season well with salt and pepper, as well as nutmeg and chilli powder to taste. Add the grated cheese and mix. Set aside to cool a little.

4. Place the chilled dough on a lightly floured work surface and knead again. Roll out the dough to be about 2–3 mm (⅛ in.) thick. Then cut out discs of approx. 10 cm (4 in.) in diameter, using a large glass or another round cutter. Knead the rest of the dough again, then roll it out and cut out more discs until all the dough has been used up.

5. Place 1–2 tsp. of the filling into the centre of each disc and fold the empanadas into a half-moon shape. Press down firmly along the edges using a fork.

Continued on the next page ▶

TOP TIP:

The empanadas taste particularly good with home-made dips like guacamole (recipe on p. 114) or cashew dip (recipe on p. 124).

You can vary the recipe really easily, by using different types of vegetable or homemade vegan cream cheese or feta, for example.

6. Transfer the empanadas to a baking sheet greased with oil (or lined with baking paper).

7. Mix together the olive oil, soya milk and a little turmeric and brush over the empanadas.

8. Bake in a preheated oven at 200°C (400°F) for approx. 20 minutes until crisp and golden.

9. The empanadas can be served hot or cold.

Crispy tofu nuggets

These crispy baked tofu nuggets taste great with barbecue sauce
and make a delicious vegan alternative to chicken nuggets.
Perfect for a night in with friends!

40 mins + 30 mins to rest
Makes 4 portions

1 block of firm tofu
 approx. 400 g (2 cups)
120 g (1 cup) breadcrumbs,
 e.g. panko
3 tbsp. olive oil
1 tsp. ground paprika
1 tsp. sea salt
½ tsp. pepper
1 tbsp. nutritional yeast
 flakes
60 g (½ cup) cornflour
120 ml (1 cup) plant milk
1 tsp. apple cider vinegar

1. Cut the tofu into 5–6 slices. Wrap in kitchen paper (or a clean tea towel) to remove any moisture. For best results, place a pan or another heavy object on top and leave for around half an hour (or preferably overnight) until the tofu is very dry. Cut the tofu slices into sticks.

2. Preheat the oven to 200°C (400°F).

3. Take three shallow dishes. Combine the breadcrumbs, olive oil, paprika, salt, pepper and yeast flakes in one dish. Place the cornflour into another dish. Mix the plant milk and apple cider vinegar in the third dish (after approx. 5 minutes the mixture will curdle to form vegan buttermilk).

4. Roll the tofu sticks in the cornflour and then dip them in the plant milk. Repeat (roll them in the cornflour again and then dip in the plant milk). Then roll the sticks in the breadcrumb mixture.

5. Place the tofu nuggets next to one another on a lightly greased baking tray, leaving a good distance between each one. Bake for 20 minutes, then turn and bake for another 15 minutes.

Continued on the
next page ▶

For the dip:
⅓ tsp. barbecue sauce
2 tbsp. vegan butter,
  melted

If needed, you can also spray the nuggets with a little oil to make them crispier and stop them from drying out.

6. While the nuggets are baking, mix the barbecue sauce together with the vegan butter.

7. After 30 minutes, remove the nuggets from the oven and brush with the barbecue sauce. Return to the oven and bake for another 5 minutes until crispy!

8. The tofu nuggets taste great with a herby dip.

Sweet potato fries

30 mins + 1 hour soaking time
Makes 1–2 portions

2 large sweet potatoes
2 tbsp. cornflour
2–3 tbsp. olive oil
ground paprika, to taste
sea salt

TOP TIP:
These fries taste really good
with vegan mayonnaise
(recipe on p. 28) or
guacamole (recipe on p. 114).

1. Peel the sweet potatoes and cut into sticks.

2. Place the sticks in a bowl, cover with cold water and leave to soak for approx. 1 hour.

3. Preheat the oven to 200°C [400°F] (fan).

4. Dry the soaked sweet potato sticks and mix well with the cornflour, oil and a little paprika.

5. Spread the sticks over a baking tray lined with baking paper and bake for approx. 20–25 minutes. Turn after 10 minutes.

6. Sprinkle with salt to taste, serve and enjoy!

Falafel with pitta and hummus

30 mins
Makes 3 portions

For the falafel:
500 g (3 cups) chickpeas (tinned or cooked)
2–3 garlic cloves
2 tbsp. breadcrumbs + 2 tbsp. flour
1 onion
a bunch of fresh parsley or coriander
ground cumin
salt and pepper
olive oil for frying
2 tbsp. sesame seeds

For the hummus:
500 g (3 cups) chickpeas (tinned or cooked)
3 garlic cloves
3 tbsp. sesame paste (tahini)
3 tbsp. olive oil
ground paprika
ground cumin
juice of ½ lemon

For the tahini and peanut sauce:
1 garlic clove
a small piece of ginger
3 tbsp. sesame paste (tahini)
1 tbsp. peanut butter
1–2 tbsp. soy sauce
1 tbsp. sugar
a squeeze of lemon or lime juice

Other:
3 pitta breads
an iceberg lettuce
1 small green pepper

To make the falafel:
1. Drain the chickpeas. Peel and finely chop the garlic. Wash and roughly chop the parsley.

2. Blend all the falafel ingredients to a purée and season with the spices. If the dough is too wet, simply work in more flour.

3. Shape the dough into small balls or patties and fry in oil until golden brown. Sprinkle the cooked falafel with sesame seeds.

To make the hummus:
1. Drain the chickpeas. Peel and finely chop the garlic.

2. Place all the ingredients in a blender and combine until the mixture has a creamy, mousse-like consistency.

To make the tahini and peanut sauce:
1. Peel and crush the garlic. Peel and finely grate the ginger.

2. Mix together all the ingredients for the tahini and peanut sauce in a bowl and season.

3. Toast the pitta breads.

4. Wash the lettuce and pepper. Slice the pepper into rings.

5. Cut open the pitta breads, drizzle in the sauce and fill with the lettuce, pepper and falafel. Serve with the hummus dip.

Potato cakes

50 mins
Makes 2 portions

3–4 medium potatoes
100 g (1 cup) carrots
1–2 tbsp. spring onions
1 tbsp. parsley, chopped
¾ tsp. salt
¼ tsp. black pepper
a pinch of ground nutmeg
35 g (¼ cup) flour
40 g (½ cup) vegan
   cheese, grated
2 tbsp. olive oil (for frying)
breadcrumbs

For the vegetable filling:
2 tsp. olive oil
1 carrot
1 garlic clove
a handful of baby spinach
2–3 tbsp. sweetcorn
salt
pepper
fresh herbs, chopped
   (optional)
3 tbsp. vegan cheese, grated

1. Boil the carrots and potatoes. Drain off the cooking water and leave to stand. Peel the potatoes and use a potato masher to mash them, together with the carrots. Leave to cool fully. Wash and chop the spring onions and parsley.

2. While the mash is cooling, prepare the vegetable filling. Heat the oil in a frying pan. Grate the carrot, peel and finely chop the garlic and wash the spinach. Place the carrot into the pan and sauté for 1 minute. Add the spinach and garlic and cook for 1–2 minutes, until the spinach is wilted. Season to taste. Rinse and drain the sweetcorn and add to the pan. Leave to cool. Stir in the vegan cheese.

3. Mix the mashed potato with the spring onions, parsley, salt, pepper and nutmeg in a large bowl. Add the flour and vegan cheese and mix well.

4. Take a handful of the potato mixture and shape into a well in the palm of your hand. Fill with the vegetable mixture and then surround the filling with potato mixture. Shape into a flat ball, coat in the breadcrumbs and press flat to make a patty.

5. Heat 2 tablespoons of oil in a frying pan over a medium heat. Fry the potato cakes for around 3–5 minutes on each side until golden brown. Serve with the cashew dip or vegan cream cheese.

Vegan classics

Kohlrabi schnitzel burger

30 mins
Makes 2

1 small to medium-sized kohlrabi
approx. 80 ml (⅓ cup) plant milk
75 g (⅔ cup) all-purpose or
    spelt flour (see also page 13)
1 tsp. cornflour
120 g (1 cup) breadcrumbs
approx. 4 tbsp. olive oil
    (for frying)
1 large tomato
2 burger buns
4 lettuce leaves
a small handful of bean sprouts
1 tbsp. ketchup
1 tsp. mustard

For the mushroom filling:
125 g (1 cup) mushrooms
1 garlic clove
1 small onion
1 tbsp. olive oil
1–2 tbsp. soy sauce

For the guacamole:
1 avocado
a squeeze of lemon
salt
pepper

1. Peel the kohlrabi and cut into four slices around 1 cm (⅓ in.) thick.

2. For the breadcrumb coating, take three deep plates. Pour the plant milk into one, mix the flour and cornflour in another and place the breadcrumbs in the third.

3. Dip the kohlrabi slices in the plant milk and then coat in the flour. Shake off some of the moisture and then dip back into the plant milk and flour. Finally, coat in the breadcrumbs and carefully press on the coating.

4. Heat the oil in a frying pan and fry the kohlrabi schnitzel for approx. 4–5 minutes on each side, until golden brown.

5. Wash, clean and slice the mushrooms. Peel and finely chop the onion and garlic. In a separate pan, heat 1 tbsp. oil and fry the mushrooms and onions for around 4 minutes. Add the garlic and fry for another minute. Finally, add the soy sauce and stir to combine.

6. Slice the tomato. Slice the burger buns and top one half of each with lettuce, two kohlrabi schnitzels, ketchup, mustard, tomato, bean sprouts, mushrooms and onion. Spoon on some guacamole and place the lid on top.

To make the guacamole:
Halve the avocado, remove the stone and spoon out the flesh. Mash with a fork and season with lemon juice, salt and pepper.

Chilli sin carne

50 mins
Makes 3–4 portions

2 onions
2–3 garlic cloves
1–2 carrots
120 g (⅔ cup) soya mince
   (or another vegan mince meat
   alternative)
400 ml (1⅔ cups) vegetable stock
2–3 tbsp. olive oil
approx. 1 tsp. ground paprika
1 small chilli, chopped finely
50 g (¼ cup) tomato purée
1 tin (400 g/2 cups) kidney beans
1 tin (400 g/2 cups) sweetcorn
1 tin (400 g/2 cups) chopped
   tomatoes
salt
pepper
a little sugar
400 g (2 cups) rice

For the topping:
sesame seeds
chilli flakes
fresh parsley
limes, quartered

1. Peel and finely chop the onion and garlic. Wash and finely dice the carrots.

2. Soak the soya mince in hot vegetable stock for 5–10 minutes and then drain.

3. Heat the oil in a hot frying pan and fry the carrot and onion.

4. Add the soya mince, paprika, chilli, garlic and tomato purée and fry briefly.

5. Drain the kidney beans and sweetcorn. Add the tomatoes, stock, kidney beans and sweetcorn to the pan and simmer for approx. 20–25 minutes over a low heat.

6. Season with salt, pepper and sugar.

7. While the chilli is simmering, cook the rice according to the packet instructions.

8. Serve the chilli with rice, chilli flakes, sesame seeds, parsley and limes.

BBQ cauliflower wings

1 hour
Makes 2 portions

1 cauliflower
180 ml (¾ cup) plant milk
3 tbsp. water
100–120 g (1⅛ cups) chickpea flour
2–3 tbsp. garlic powder
1 tbsp. olive oil
¼ tsp. salt
¼ tsp. sweet ground paprika
250 g (1 cup) barbecue sauce

For the barbecue sauce:
250 g (1 cup) ketchup
2–3 tbsp. brown sugar
3 tbsp. water
2 tbsp. apple cider vinegar
2 tbsp. Worcester sauce
  or soy sauce
a dash of hot chilli sauce
  or Tabasco
1 tsp. sweet ground paprika
½ tsp. garlic powder
1 tsp. mustard powder
salt

1. Preheat the oven to 220°C (425°F). Line a baking tray with baking paper.

2. Wash the cauliflower and divide into florets.

3. Place the milk, water, flour and spices into a bowl and combine to form a thick batter.

4. Coat each cauliflower floret in the batter, shake off any excess batter and lay the florets on the baking sheet.

5. Bake the florets for approx. 20 minutes until golden brown. Turn the florets after 10 minutes, so that they turn golden brown and crispy on all sides.

6. While the cauliflower is baking, prepare the barbecue sauce: Place all the sauce ingredients into a saucepan, bring to the boil and then leave to simmer over a low heat for approx. 10 minutes, stirring occasionally. If the sauce is too thick, add a little more water. (If you like it spicy, simply add more Tabasco.)

7. Leave the sauce to cool. For the marinade, combine 1 cup of the barbecue sauce with 1 tbsp. oil. Once the cauliflower is cooked, remove from the oven and evenly coat the florets with the barbecue sauce marinade.

8. Return the cauliflower to the oven and bake for another 20 minutes.

9. Serve the cauliflower wings with rice or any of your favourite dips.

Pasta Bolognese

30 mins
Makes 2 portions

1 onion
2 garlic cloves
100 g (1 cup) carrots
100 g (1 cup) celery
200 g (1 cup) firm tofu
2 tbsp. olive oil
200 g (1 cup) passata
1 tbsp. tomato purée
200 g (1 cup) chopped tomatoes
2 tsp. dried Italian herbs
1 tsp. raw cane sugar
salt
pepper
vegetable stock, as required
250 g (approx. 8 oz) of your
    preferred pasta
nutritional yeast flakes
fresh basil

1. Peel and finely chop the onion and garlic. Finely dice the carrots and celery.

2. Squeeze out the moisture from the tofu (for best results, use kitchen paper) and break into breadcrumbs.

3. Heat the olive oil in a non-stick frying pan and fry the tofu over a high heat until it's nice and golden.

4. Add the onion, carrots and celery and fry until the onions are translucent.

5. Add the garlic and fry for approx. 30 seconds.

6. Stir in the passata, tomato purée and chopped tomatoes.

7. Season the sauce with the herbs, sugar, salt and pepper and simmer over a medium heat for around 15–20 minutes until the sauce has thickened (if it gets too thick, add a little vegetable stock).

8. While the sauce is cooking, boil the pasta in salted water until al dente and then drain.

9. Serve the pasta with the sauce. If you like, you can also sprinkle over some yeast flakes and basil.

Spinach quesadillas

40 mins
Makes 4–6

1 onion
2 garlic cloves
250 g (8 cups) fresh
 spinach
1–2 tbsp. olive oil
salt
pepper
chilli flakes

For the quesadillas:
approx. 250 g (2 cups)
 vegan mozzarella
 (recipe on p. 22)
3 tsp. olive oil
4–6 tortilla wraps (approx.
 19.5 cm [7½ in.]
 diameter)
150 g (1¾ cups) vegan
 cheese

1. Peel and finely chop the onion and garlic. Rinse and drain the spinach, and sauté for 1–2 minutes, or until wilted.

2. Heat the oil in a frying pan. Add the onion and garlic and sweat until translucent. Add the spinach and fry until wilted. Season with salt, pepper and chilli flakes.

To make the quesadillas:
1. Combine the spinach mixture with the mozzarella.

2. Heat a frying pan over a medium heat and brush with oil.

3. Place the tortilla in the pan. Evenly spread around 3 tbsp. of the filling onto the tortilla, leaving a narrow gap around the edge. Sprinkle with vegan cheese. Place another tortilla over the filling. Using a turner, gently press down the tortillas so that everything sticks together.

4. Fry the tortilla for approx. 2–3 minutes, carefully turn it over and fry on the other side until crisp and golden.

5. Repeat steps 3 and 4 with the rest of the filling and as many tortillas as needed (approx. 4–6, depending on the size).

6. Place the cooked tortillas on a chopping board and use a sharp knife or pizza cutter to slice them into three pieces.

7. Serve warm with guacamole or other dips of your choice.

Leek and spinach quiche

55 mins
Makes 1 quiche
(20–22 cm/7–9 in.)

1 tbsp. ground flax seeds
80 g (⅓ cup) soft vegan
  butter
190 g (1½ cups) flour
a pinch of salt
a pinch of turmeric
2 tbsp. plant-based cream
1 tbsp. olive oil
½ leek (only the pale
  green or white part)
350 g (10 cups) fresh
  spinach
350 g (2⅓ cups) silken tofu
1 tbsp. chickpea flour
2–3 tbsp. nutritional yeast
  flakes
1 tsp. salt
½ tsp. pepper
¼ tsp. turmeric
¾ tsp. garlic powder
125 g (1½ cups) vegan
  cheese

For the topping:
pine nuts

1. Stir the ground flax seeds into 3 tbsp. hot water and leave to soak for approx. 5 minutes.

2. Combine the flour and salt in a large bowl. Cut the vegan butter into cubes and add to the flour, along with the flax seeds.

3. Using your hands, knead to form a dough. Transfer the dough to a work surface and continue to knead until it's nice and smooth. Shape the dough into a ball and flatten slightly. Wrap in cling film and place in the fridge to chill for 30 minutes.

4. Once chilled, transfer the dough to a floured surface and roll out to a thickness of 1 mm (⅕ in.) before placing in a lightly greased tin (25 cm [10 in.] diameter). Using a fork, prick the base in a few places.

5. Preheat the oven to 220°C (425°F).

6. To make the spinach mixture, heat the oil in a large frying pan. Wash and finely chop the leek, add to the pan and fry for around 3 minutes until lightly browned and soft. Rinse and drain the spinach, and sauté for 1–2 minutes or until wilted and add to the pan, frying for approx. 2 minutes until the spinach is wilted.

7. Transfer the wilted spinach to a sieve and drain. Press well to remove any excess moisture. If required, wrap in kitchen paper and press again to remove as much moisture as possible.

Continued on the next page ▶

TOP TIP:

For a crispier shortcrust, cover the pastry case with dried beans or chickpeas (so that it doesn't collapse while baking) and blind-bake for approx. 10 minutes. Then reduce the temperature to 180°C (350°F), remove the beans, add the filling and bake for a further 30–40 minutes.

8. Place the tofu, chickpea flour, yeast flakes and spices into a blender and blend until creamy.

9. Add the spinach and mix well. Crumble the vegan cheese and stir into the mixture. If required, add more seasoning.

10. Transfer the filling to the pastry-lined tin and smooth over the top.

11. Bake the quiche for 10 minutes, then reduce the temperature to 180°C (350°F) and bake for a further 30–40 minutes, until the filling has set and the top is golden brown. If the edges dry out too much while baking, you can add shine by brushing them with a little vegan cream. If they start to get too dark, loosely cover the top of the quiche with a piece of foil or baking paper.

12. Leave the quiche to cool for approx. 10 minutes before slicing and serve sprinkled with toasted pine nuts.

Spaghetti carbonara with coconut bacon

40 mins + 8 hours soaking time
Makes 4 portions

200 g (1⅓ cups) cashew nuts or
    blanched almonds
150 g (1 cup) frozen peas
400 ml (1⅔ cups) water
2 tsp. vegetable stock powder
3–4 tbsp. nutritional yeast flakes
500 g (1lb) spaghetti
1 tbsp. olive oil + a little extra
    for drizzling
3–4 garlic cloves
400 g (3¼ cups) mushrooms
salt
pepper

1. Cover the cashew nuts with water and leave to soak overnight. Alternatively, you can simply boil them for 15 minutes. Defrost the peas. Drain the cashews, rinse them with fresh water and transfer to a blender with 200 ml (¾ cup) of the water, the vegetable stock powder and yeast flakes, and blend until creamy. Add the rest of the water to form a cashew cream.

2. Cook the spaghetti according to the packet instructions, and then drain well. Return to the pan and stir in a little olive oil so that the pasta doesn't stick together.

3. While the pasta is cooking, peel and finely chop the garlic and wash, clean and slice the mushrooms. Heat the olive oil in a frying pan and fry the mushrooms until golden brown (approx. 7–8 minutes). Add the garlic and fry for another minute.

4. Add the cashew nut cream, pasta and peas to the pan of mushrooms and give everything a good stir. If the sauce is too thick, add a little water or milk (for more creaminess). If it's too thin, cook a little longer to reduce. Season with salt and pepper.

5. Serve the spaghetti carbonara hot with coconut bacon and enjoy!

Continued on the next page ▶

For the coconut bacon:
4 tsp. tamari or soy sauce
1 tsp. liquid smoke or
more tamari sauce
2 tsp. maple syrup
2 tsp. olive oil
1 tsp. ground paprika
60 g (¾ cup) unsweetened
coconut flakes

To make the coconut bacon:
1. Preheat the oven to 160°C (325°F) and line a baking tray with baking paper.

2. In a large bowl, mix together the tamari, liquid smoke, maple syrup, oil and paprika. Add the coconut flakes and mix well. Set aside to marinate.

3. Spread the coconut flakes evenly over the lined baking tray and bake for approx. 15 minutes until they dry out and turn golden brown.

4. Remove from the oven and leave to cool completely. The coconut bacon will keep for at least a week in an air-tight container.

Mac and cheese

This creamy mac and cheese is not only vegan,
it's also really healthy and tastes delicious.

20 mins + 4 hours soaking time
Makes 4 portions

80 g (⅔ cup) cashew nuts, soaked
    in water (or cashew butter)
400 g (approx. 14 oz.) of your
    preferred pasta
2 medium potatoes
1–2 carrots
1 onion
2–3 garlic cloves
1 tsp. olive oil
3–4 tbsp. nutritional yeast flakes
1 tbsp. lemon juice
½ tbsp. mustard
1 tsp. ground paprika
salt
pepper

For the topping:
vegan parmesan (recipe on p. 20)
fresh parsley
mushrooms

1. Soak the cashew nuts for at least 4 hours (or preferably overnight). If you're short on time, you can simply boil them for 10–15 minutes instead. Drain and rinse.

2. Follow the instructions on the packet to cook the pasta al dente. While the pasta is cooking, prepare the cheese sauce.

3. Peel the potatoes, carrots and onion, roughly chop and cook in a pan of boiling water for around 10 minutes (or until the vegetables are soft). Peel and finely chop the garlic. Heat the olive oil in a small frying pan and fry the garlic for approx. 1–2 minutes.

4. Once the vegetables are cooked, remove them from the pan with a slotted spoon and transfer to a blender along with approx. 175 ml (¾ cup) of the cooking liquid (from the vegetables), the garlic, the soaked cashews, yeast flakes, lemon juice, mustard and spices. Blend until creamy. If the mixture is too thick, add a little more of the cooking liquid.

5. Drain the pasta, then return it to the pan, pour over the cheese sauce and warm it up, stirring occasionally.

6. If needed, add more seasoning and serve sprinkled with vegan parmesan, mushrooms and chopped parsley.

TOP TIP:
You can transfer the vegan cheese sauce to a sealed jar and keep it in the fridge for approx. 3–4 days. It also freezes well. Another option is to fill an ovenproof dish with the mac and cheese, sprinkle it with breadcrumbs and bake in the oven at 180°C (350°F) for around 10–15 minutes.

Spinach pizza with mushrooms and garlic

1 hour + 1 hour to prove
Makes 1 pizza

175 ml (¾ cup) lukewarm water
10 g yeast (¼ cube)
1 tsp. sugar
250 g (2 cups) flour
1 tsp. salt
1–2 tbsp. olive oil

For the topping:
200 g (6 cups) fresh spinach
3 garlic cloves
1 tbsp. olive oil
salt
pepper
150 g (⅔ cup) vegan cream
   cheese
75 g (1 cup) vegan cheese, grated
150 g (1¼ cups) mushrooms
1 tbsp. olive oil
2 tbsp. pine nuts to garnish

TOP TIP:
For a softer dough, simply replace the water with plant milk.

1. Mix together the water, yeast and sugar and leave to stand for 5 minutes. Combine the flour and salt in a large bowl. Make a well in the middle, pour in the olive oil and gradually work it into the flour, starting at the edges.

2. Add the yeast mixture and knead thoroughly for at least 10 minutes. Leave the dough to prove for around 10 minutes and then knead well again, using your hands. Cover the dough and leave in a warm place to prove for another hour.

3. Using a rolling pin, roll out the pizza dough and place on a baking sheet lined with baking paper. (You can also use a pizza tray or a pizza stone, as long as it's no higher than 1.5 cm [½ in.]). Preheat the oven to 200°C (400°F).

4. Place the spinach in a saucepan, cover with boiling water and cook for 1–2 minutes. Squeeze out any excess moisture and roughly chop.

5. Peel and finely chop the garlic. Heat a little oil in a small frying pan and fry the garlic for approx. 30 seconds, stirring continuously. Add the cream cheese and spinach. Season with salt and pepper and stir.

6. Spread the spinach mixture over the pizza base and sprinkle with vegan cheese. Bake for approx. 10–15 minutes until the cheese has melted.

7. While the pizza is baking, fry the mushrooms in the oil for around 6–8 minutes until golden brown. Season with a little salt.

8. Toast the pine nuts in a dry frying pan.

9. As soon as the pizza is ready, arrange the mushrooms on top and sprinkle with pine nuts.

Spinach ravioli with mushrooms

20 mins
Makes 17

150 g (1¼ cups) all-purpose
  or light spelt flour
  (see also page 13)
150 g (¾ cup) semolina
  (or pasta flour or add more
  all-purpose flour)
½ tsp. salt
150 ml (⅔ cup) water
2 tsp. olive oil

For the spinach filling:
200 g (6 cups) frozen spinach
50 g (½ cup) vegan parmesan
  (recipe on p. 20), grated
100 g (½ cup) vegan cream
  cheese or cashew ricotta
  (recipe on p. 18)
salt
pepper

1. Mix the flour with the semolina and salt and make a pile on the work surface with a well in the middle. Pour the water and olive oil into the middle and knead everything into a smooth dough.

2. Shape the dough into a ball, wrap in cling film and place in the fridge to chill for at least half an hour.

3. Defrost the spinach, squeeze out any excess moisture and roughly chop.

4. Add the vegan parmesan and cream cheese. Mix well and season with salt and pepper. (If the filling is too dry, add a little vegan cream or plant milk.)

5. Roll the pasta dough out thinly on a lightly floured work surface. Use a circular utensil such as a jar or biscuit cutter to cut the dough into discs (approx. 7.5 cm [3 in.] diameter).

6. Spoon approx. 1 tbsp. of the spinach mixture into the centre of each disc. Brush the edges with a little water and fold the disc in half. Pinch the edges together with your fingers and then press with a fork.

7. Bring a large pan of salted water to the boil. Slide the ravioli into the water and simmer for 3–4 minutes until they float to the surface.

8. Remove from the water with a slotted spoon and drain well.

Continued on the
next page ▶

For the mushrooms:
2 garlic cloves
300 g (2½ cups)
   mushrooms
1 tbsp. olive oil
2–3 tbsp. soy sauce

9. Peel and finely chop the garlic. Wash, clean and slice the mushrooms.

10. Heat the olive oil in a frying pan and fry the mushrooms over a high heat for around 3 minutes until they are lightly browned. Add the chopped garlic and fry for around 30 seconds.

11. Douse with the soy sauce, reduce the heat and fry for a further 2–3 minutes.

12. Drain the ravioli, shake off any excess water, season with salt and pepper and serve.

Vegetable pasta pockets

1½ hours + 30 mins
to chill
Makes 10

125 g (1 cup) all-purpose
    or light spelt flour
    (see also page 13)
125 g (⅔ cup) semolina
    (or pasta flour or add
    more all-purpose flour)
½ tsp. salt
120 ml (½ cup) water
2 tsp. olive oil

For the filling:
1–2 medium potatoes
100 g (1 cup) frozen peas
3 tbsp. pine nuts
1 tsp. olive oil for frying
1 small onion
2 garlic cloves
200 g (6 cups) baby
    spinach
2–3 tbsp. vegan cream
    cheese or cashew ricotta
    (recipe on p. 18)
2 tbsp. nutritional yeast
    flakes
salt
pepper
2 tbsp. vegan butter
fresh herbs and pine nuts
    to garnish

1. Defrost the peas.

2. Mix the flour, semolina and salt in a bowl and make a pile with a well in the middle. Pour in the water and olive oil and knead everything into a smooth dough, using your hands.

3. Shape the dough into a ball, flatten slightly and wrap in cling film. Place in the fridge to chill for around half an hour.

4. Peel the potatoes, cut into quarters and cook in a pan of salted water for approx. 20 minutes (depending on size) until soft. Drain off the cooking liquid and set the pan aside, uncovered, to allow the rest of the water to evaporate.

5. Toast the pine nuts in a dry frying pan.

6. Add the defrosted peas and the pine nuts. Mash everything to a purée using a potato masher.

7. Heat the oil in a frying pan and sweat the onion for 1–2 minutes. Add the garlic and spinach and fry for another 1–2 minutes until the spinach is wilted. Squeeze out any excess moisture.

8. Roughly chop the spinach mixture and add to the pea and potato purée along with the vegan cream cheese. Mix well and season to taste with yeast flakes, salt and pepper.

Continued on the next page ▶

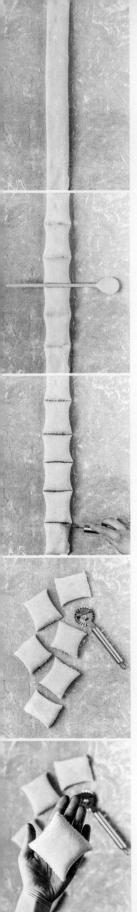

9. On a floured surface, roll out the pasta dough thinly using a rolling pin to form a long rectangle.

10. Spread the vegetable mixture onto the pasta dough, leaving a border around all sides (approx. 1.5–2 cm [½–¾ in.]). Brush the edge on one side with a little water so that you can seal the pockets better. Roll the dough into a long wrap. (The fold should be facing down.)

11. Divide the roll into 6–8 equally-sized pockets by pressing down carefully with the handle of a wooden spoon. Separate the pockets using a pizza cutter or sharp knife.

12. Bring a large pan of salted water or vegetable stock to the boil. Slide the pockets into the water and cook for approx. 15 minutes (reduce the heat to a simmer rather than a rolling boil). Remove from the water with a ladle and drain well.

13. The pockets can either be used as an accompaniment to a vegetable soup, served with a sauce or fried until crispy.

14. To fry them, heat the vegan butter in a frying pan over a medium heat. Transfer the pockets to the pan and fry for approx. 5 minutes on each side, until crisp and golden.

15. Garnish with herbs and pine nuts. This dish tastes great with garlic mushrooms, roasted tomatoes or other vegetables.

Vegetable dumplings

These dumplings, also known as gyoza, are filled and
fried Japanese dough pockets. I've come up with a vegan version
of this delicious Asian dish, and I'm delighted to share it with you.

1 hour
Makes 4 portions

300 g (2⅓ cups) all-purpose
   or light spelt flour
   (see also page 13)
½ tsp. salt
150 ml (⅔ cup) hot water
a little cornflour or flour
   for dusting
1–2 tbsp. sesame oil

For the vegetable filling:
1 onion
2 garlic cloves
1 tbsp. ginger
100 g (1 cup) carrots
200 g (1⅔ cups)
   mushrooms
½ leek
200 g (2 cups) cabbage
salt
2 tbsp. soy sauce
1 tbsp. rice wine vinegar
pepper
1 tsp. sriracha or sambal
   oelek

1. Mix together the flour and salt in a bowl. Add the
water, stirring continuously. Transfer the dough to a
work surface and knead for around 3–5 minutes to
form a smooth, soft dough. Shape the dough into a
ball, wrap in cling film and place in the fridge to chill
for 30 minutes.

2. Divide the dough into two halves (this makes it
easier to roll out). Dust the work surface with a little
cornflour and roll out the dough to a thickness of
approx. 2 mm (¼ in.).

3. Using a jar or biscuit cutter, cut out 8 cm (3 in.)
discs.

4. Gather up the leftover dough and knead into
a new ball. Roll out and cut out more discs. Before
stacking them up, dust the discs with a little
cornflour to stop them from sticking together.

5. The dumplings will dry out quickly, so use them
straight away, store them in the fridge in an air-tight
container or freeze them.

Continued on the
next page ▶

For the sauce:

3 tbsp. soy sauce
1 tbsp. rice wine vinegar
1 tbsp. agave syrup
¼ tsp. sesame oil
½ tsp. sriracha
   or sambal oelek

For the topping:

1 tbsp. toasted sesame
   seeds
2 tbsp. spring onions,
   chopped into rings

6. Place a heaped teaspoon of the filling onto the centre of each disc. Moisten the outer edges with water and form the dumplings into a fan shape. Seal the dumplings tightly.

7. Repeat this process until the dough has been used up.

8. Heat the oil in a frying pan over a medium heat. Transfer the dumplings to the pan and fry for 2–3 minutes or until the bottoms are well browned. Pour in around 3 tbsp. water and cover with a lid. Steam for 7–8 minutes or until the water has evaporated.

9. Combine all the ingredients for the sauce.

10. Sprinkle the dumplings with sesame seeds and spring onions and serve with the sauce.

To make the vegetable filling:

1. Peel and finely chop the onion, garlic, ginger and carrot. Wash the mushrooms, leek and cabbage and finely chop. Heat the oil in a large frying pan.

2. Add the mushrooms, onion and carrots and fry for 2–3 minutes until they are lightly browned. Add the leek and cabbage, along with a little salt, and sweat for a further 5–7 minutes, stirring occasionally, until the vegetables have softened and cooked through. If the pan starts to dry out, add a little water. Add the garlic, ginger and the rest of the ingredients for the filling. Fry for a minute longer to bring out the flavours.

3. Leave to cool.

Sushi

Sushi is usually associated with raw fish, but you can also make
a really tasty vegan version!

30 mins
Makes 3 rolls and
5 sandwiches

250 g (1⅓ cups) sushi rice
1–2 tbsp. rice wine vinegar
1 tbsp. sugar
½ tsp. salt
6 sheets of nori

For the filling:
a handful of spinach
50 g (¼ cup) vegan cream
   cheese, with herbs
1 avocado
pepper
half a mango
12 sun-dried tomatoes
25 g (¼ cup) walnuts

1. Cook the sushi rice in a pan according to the
packet instructions. Reduce to a low heat, place
the lid on the pan and leave to simmer for approx.
10–15 minutes. Remove the pan from the heat,
remove the lid and leave the rice to stand for
approx. 5 minutes, allowing any excess water
to evaporate. Transfer the rice to a large dish,
spread out and leave to cool.

2. Combine the rice wine vinegar, sugar and salt in
a small saucepan and boil until the salt and sugar have
dissolved. Leave to cool and then fold into the rice.

3. Wash and drain the spinach. Halve the avocado
and remove the stone. Scoop out the flesh with a
spoon and cut into thin slices. Season with a little salt
and pepper. Peel the mango, remove the flesh from
the stone and cut into slices. Finely chop the sun-dried
tomatoes.

4. Lightly toast the walnuts in a dry frying pan.

To make the sushi rolls:
5. Cover a sushi mat with cling film and place a sheet
of nori on top.

6. Spread the rice out evenly onto the sheet, leaving
1–2 cm (⅓–⅔ in.) uncovered at the top and bottom.

Continued on the
next page ▶

7. Top with your preferred fillings. Dampen the uncovered ends with a little water and, using the sushi mat to help you, roll it all up tightly.

8. Using a wet knife, slice the roll into equally-sized pieces.

9. Repeat this process with another nori sheet.

To make the sushi sandwiches:

10. Lay a sheet of nori onto a sushi mat or a piece of foil. Spoon 1–2 tablespoons of rice into the centre of the sheet and flatten slightly. Cover with fillings of your choice (cream cheese, spinach, avocado, mango, tomatoes or walnuts). Top with another layer of rice.

11. Carefully fold the corners into the centre and work them over each other with wet fingers.

12. Turn the sushi sandwich over, shape it a little and leave to stand for a few minutes before slicing into two halves.

13. Repeat this process with 3 more nori sheets.

Light meals

Lentil dahl

35 mins
Makes 2 portions

1 small onion
2 garlic cloves
a small piece of ginger
1 tbsp. vegan butter or olive oil
½ tsp. turmeric
½ tsp. coriander
½ tsp. cumin
½ tsp. ground paprika
¼ tsp. garam masala
350 ml (1½ cups) vegetable stock
150 g (¾ cup) red lentils
125 ml (½ cup) coconut milk
juice of ½ lemon
salt
pepper
a little sugar

For the topping:
fresh parsley
cashew nuts
chilli, chopped into rings

1. Peel and finely chop the onion, garlic and ginger.

2. Heat the butter in a saucepan and add the onion, garlic, ginger and spices. Sweat for around 5 minutes.

3. Add the vegetable stock and lentils, bring to the boil, then reduce the heat and simmer for approx. 15–20 minutes.

4. Once the lentils have absorbed most of the stock, stir in the coconut milk.

5. Season with the lemon juice, pepper, salt and sugar and continue to simmer for around 10 minutes until the lentils have softened. If the sauce is too thick, add a little more water or coconut milk.

6. Garnish with parsley, cashew nuts and chilli to taste.

7. Serve the dahl with freshly baked naan bread or rice, or enjoy it on its own.

Stuffed sweet potato skins with avocado aioli

1½ hours

Makes 4 portions

3 tbsp. olive oil
4–5 medium sized sweet
   potatoes
1 onion
half a red pepper
2 garlic cloves
1 tin (400 g/1¾ cups)
   black beans
1 tin (400 g/1¾ cups)
   sweetcorn
salt
pepper
a pinch of chilli powder
3–4 tbsp. salsa
approx. 120 g (1½ cups)
   vegan cheese, grated

For the aioli:
1 avocado
1–2 tbsp. vegan mayonnaise
1–2 garlic cloves
1 tsp. lemon juice

Continued on the
next page ▶

1. Preheat the oven to 220°C (425°F) and brush a baking tray with a little oil.

2. Using a fork, prick the sweet potatoes in several places and transfer to the baking tray. Bake for around 40–50 minutes until they are soft. (It's a good idea to stick a fork into the potatoes after 40 minutes to see if they're ready.) Quick version: Wrap the pricked potatoes in a tea towel and cook in the microwave for approx. 10 minutes.

3. Finely chop the onion, pepper and garlic. Rinse and drain the beans and sweetcorn. Heat the oil in a frying pan. Add the onion and pepper and fry for approx. 3–5 minutes until soft and brown. Add the garlic and fry for another minute until fragrant. Season with salt and chilli powder. Set aside.

4. Once the sweet potatoes are soft, remove from the oven and leave to cool for around 5 minutes. Leave the oven on for now. Cut the sweet potatoes into two halves and scoop out the centres with a spoon, leaving a thin layer of potato (approx. 1 cm/⅓ in.) in the skin. Transfer the sweet potato flesh to a bowl and mash with a fork. Add the onion mix, beans, sweetcorn and salsa and mix well.

For the topping:
fresh parsley or coriander
spring onions
a squeeze of lime juice

5. Brush the edges of the potato skins with a little oil. Spoon in the filling and sprinkle with vegan cheese.

6. Bake for around 5–10 minutes or until the cheese has melted.

7. Roughly chop the parsley or coriander and slice the spring onions into rings. Drizzle some lime juice over the top.

8. Halve the avocado and remove the stone. Scoop out the flesh. Add the rest of the ingredients for the aioli and blend until creamy. Season to taste and serve with the stuffed potato skins.

Chinese pancakes with spring onions

Spring onion pancakes are a very popular dish in China.
They're made using a unique method and just three main ingredients,
and taste a bit like a thin, crispy fried flatbread.

35 mins + 30 mins to rest
Makes 4

240 g (1⅔ cups) flour
¾ tsp. salt
180 ml (¾ cup) warm
   water
4 tbsp. plant oil + a little
   extra for brushing
approx. 6 spring onions,
   with the green part
   finely chopped
sauce for dipping (dumpling
   sauce recipe on p. 170)

1. Combine the flour and salt in a large bowl. Add the water and mix using a stick blender or a fork, until all the water has combined well with the flour.

2. Knead the dough using your hands (if the dough is very dry, add approx. 1–2 tbsp. water). Transfer the dough to a work surface and continue to knead for around 5 minutes until it's soft and smooth.

3. Shape the dough into a ball and wrap in cling film or a damp cloth. Leave to rest for approx. 20–30 minutes.

4. Once rested, cut the ball of dough into four equally-sized pieces and shape into smaller balls.

5. Take one small ball of dough (keep the other three covered so that they don't dry out) and roll it out thinly on a lightly floured work surface using a rolling pin. Brush the surface with a little oil and spread spring onions on top. Roll the dough up like a wrap. Bend the roll into a spiral.

Continued on the next page ▶

6. Flatten the spiral slightly with your hands, then roll it out flat using a rolling pin (to a diameter of approx. 20–22 cm/7–9 in.).

7. Repeat this process with the remaining pieces of dough. (If you stack the pancakes up, place a piece of baking paper between each one, so that they don't stick together.)

8. Heat 1 tbsp. oil per pancake in a frying pan over a medium heat and fry for 2–3 minutes on each side until crisp and golden.

9. Once cooked, slice the spring onion pancakes into four quarters and serve hot with the dipping sauce.

Creamy polenta

15 mins
Makes 2 portions

200 ml (¾ cup) coconut milk
300 ml (1¼ cups) vegetable stock
150 g (1 cup) polenta
2–3 tbsp. nutritional yeast flakes

For the vegetable topping:
1 onion
2 garlic cloves
200 g (⅔ cup) your preferred
   mushrooms
1–2 tbsp. soy sauce
200 g (6 cups) fresh spinach
1 tbsp. olive oil
salt
pepper
a squeeze of lime juice
2–3 tbsp. pine nuts

1. Bring the coconut milk and vegetable stock to the boil in a saucepan. Use a whisk to mix in the polenta. Continue to whisk for around 1–2 minutes to prevent lumps. Reduce to a low heat.

2. Place the lid on the pan and leave the polenta for around 10 minutes (or time stated in the packet instructions) to soak up all the liquid, stirring occasionally. If the polenta gets too thick, stir in a little more coconut milk or water.

3. The polenta is ready as soon as it's nice and creamy. Lastly, stir in the yeast flakes.

4. Peel and finely chop the onion and garlic. Wash, clean and slice the mushrooms. Wash, drain and sauté the spinach for 1–2 minutes, or until wilted. Heat the oil in a frying pan. Add the mushrooms and onions and fry over a high heat for approx. 3 minutes, until lightly browned.

5. Add the garlic and fry for around 30 seconds. Douse with the soy sauce. Reduce the heat, add the spinach and fry for a further 1–2 minutes until the spinach is wilted. Season with salt, pepper and lime juice.

6. Toast the pine nuts in a small dry frying pan.

7. Serve the polenta immediately, with the mushrooms, spinach and pine nuts, while it's still warm and creamy.

Crispy baked cauliflower

This roasted cauliflower with a crispy breadcrumb coating is easy to prepare and makes a delicious and healthy alternative to the usual nuggets. The perfect side for any dish or just as a tasty snack!

50 mins
Makes 4 portions

½ head of cauliflower
2 tbsp. flour
60 ml (¼ cup) plant milk
50 g (½ cup) breadcrumbs
2–4 tbsp. nutritional yeast flakes
salt
olive oil or rapeseed oil
  to spray/drizzle

1. Preheat the oven to 200°C (400°F).

2. Wash the cauliflower and divide into florets.

3. Mix together the flour and milk in a large bowl to form a batter.

4. In a separate bowl, combine the breadcrumbs, yeast flakes and salt.

5. Dip the cauliflower florets into the batter and then roll in the breadcrumb mixture so that they're evenly coated with breadcrumbs.

6. Transfer the florets to a baking tray lined with baking paper, leaving a little space between each one. Drizzle or spray with olive oil.

7. Bake for around 30–40 minutes, until the cauliflower is golden brown and crispy.

8. Once the cauliflower is ready, serve with dips or simply enjoy on its own.

Couscous salad with roasted chickpeas

30 mins
Makes 4 portions

125 g (¾ cup) couscous
½ cucumber
1 red pepper
250 g (1¼ cups) cherry tomatoes
80 g (½ cup) kalamata olives
a small bunch of parsley

For the crispy chickpeas:
1 tin (400 g/2 cups) chickpeas
1 tbsp. olive oil
½ tsp. ground paprika
¼ tsp. cayenne pepper
salt

For the tahini dressing:
1 garlic clove
4 tbsp. sesame paste (tahini)
2 tbsp. lemon juice
1 tsp. mustard
1 tsp. mixed, dried herbs
1–2 tsp. agave syrup
3–4 tbsp. water
salt and pepper

For the topping:
vegan feta
fresh limes

To make the crispy chickpeas:
1. Preheat the oven to 200°C (400°F). Line a baking tray with baking paper.

2. Drain and rinse the chickpeas and pat them dry. Place them in a bowl with the olive oil and spices and mix well so that the chickpeas are evenly coated.

3. Spread the chickpeas out on a baking tray and bake for around 25–30 minutes, turning occasionally, until they're nice and crispy. Leave to cool.

To make the couscous salad:
1. Prepare the couscous using vegetable stock according to the packet instructions.

2. Once it's ready, transfer the couscous to a large bowl and leave to cool.

3. While the couscous is cooking, prepare the vegetables. Wash the cucumber, pepper and tomatoes and finely chop. Chop the parsley and remove the stones from the olives, unless they are already pitted.

To make the tahini dressing:
1. Peel and crush the garlic. Combine all the ingredients for the dressing. Add more seasoning, if required.

2. Spoon the couscous into four dishes. Add the vegetables and sprinkle the chickpeas on top. Garnish with vegan feta and season with freshly squeezed lime juice, salt and pepper to taste. Serve the salad with the tahini dressing and enjoy!

Pumpkin and coconut soup

50 mins
Makes 4 portions

1 pumpkin or butternut squash
   (approx. 1 kg/2.2 lbs)
1 small sweet potato
   (approx. 250 g/8.8 oz)
1 tbsp. olive oil
1 tbsp. coconut oil
1 onion
2 garlic cloves
a small piece of ginger (15 g/½ oz)
1 tsp. sweet ground paprika
½ tsp. turmeric
½ tsp. coriander
salt
pepper
480 ml (2 cups) vegetable stock
1 tin (400 ml, 1⅔ cups)
   coconut milk

For the topping (as preferred):
peanuts
pumpkin seeds
parsley, chopped
coconut cream

1. Preheat the oven to 200°C (400°F).

2. Halve the pumpkin/squash and scoop out the seeds with a spoon. Chop each half into quarters. Using a fork, prick the sweet potato in several places. Brush the pumpkin/squash and sweet potato with a little olive oil and lay on a baking tray lined with baking paper. Bake for around 40 minutes until the flesh of the pumpkin/squash and the sweet potato are soft.

3. Peel and finely chop the onion, garlic and ginger. Heat the coconut oil in a large saucepan over a medium heat and sweat the onions for around 6–8 minutes. Add the garlic and ginger and fry for another minute, stirring continuously.

4. Once soft, peel the sweet potato and transfer to the pan, along with the soft pumpkin/squash. Pour over the stock and coconut milk. Bring to the boil, then reduce the heat and let it simmer for 5–10 minutes to bring out the flavours.

5. Remove the soup from the hob and either purée in the pan with a stick blender or transfer the soup to a blender in batches and blend until creamy.

6. If needed, add more seasoning. If the soup is too thick, add a little more stock.

7. Serve the soup garnished with peanuts, pumpkin seeds, parsley or a dollop of coconut cream.

Thai peanut ramen soup

This simple Japanese soup is made using an exceptionally creamy peanut and coconut stock, fried mushrooms and crispy tofu. Not only is it delicious, fragrant and healthy, it's also really quick and easy to make!

35 mins
Makes 4 portions

300 g (2½ cups) mushrooms
200 g (1⅓ cups) Padrón peppers
3 spring onions
2 tsp. coconut oil
2 garlic cloves
approx. 1 tsp. ground ginger
1 tbsp. Thai curry paste
1 tin (400 ml, 1¾ cups)
  coconut milk
750–1000 ml (3–4 cups)
  vegetable stock
80 g (⅓ cup) smooth peanut butter
3 tbsp. soy sauce or tamari
1 tbsp. agave syrup
a little lime juice
1 tsp. dried jalapeños
250 g (1 cup) ramen noodles
300 g (1½ cups) firm tofu
½ tsp. turmeric
2 tsp. cornflour
2 tbsp. peanut oil
350 g (2¾ cups) mushrooms
1 tbsp. soy sauce (for dousing
  the mushrooms)

For the topping (optional):
roasted peanuts
sesame seeds
spring onions, parsley
  or other herbs

1. Wash and slice the mushrooms, peppers and spring onions. Heat the coconut oil in a large saucepan. Peel and finely chop the garlic and ginger. Fry the garlic and ginger for approx. 1–2 minutes, stirring continuously. Add the curry paste and sweat for a short while. Add the sliced vegetables and fry briefly.

2. Pour in the coconut milk and stock and bring to the boil. Stir in the peanut butter, 2 tbsp. soy sauce, agave syrup, lime juice and dried jalapeños. Leave the soup to simmer for about 10 minutes. Add the noodles and cook for 5 minutes (or the time specified on the packet).

3. While the soup is cooking, drain the tofu, wrap it in kitchen paper and squeeze out any excess moisture. Cut into cubes and coat with the turmeric and a little cornflour. (This makes the tofu crispier.)

4. Heat 1 tbsp. peanut oil in two frying pans (or 2 tbsp. in one large pan). In one pan, fry the tofu on all sides until crispy. Wash and slice the mushrooms and fry in the other pan until golden brown. Add the mushrooms to the tofu, douse with 1 tbsp. soy sauce and toss the pan so that everything has a nice brown colour.

5. Once the noodle soup is ready, serve with the crispy fried tofu and the mushrooms. Chop the spring onions and sprinkle over the soup along with peanuts, sesame seeds or any other of your favourite toppings.

Hasselback potatoes

55 mins
Makes 3 portions

3–4 medium potatoes
your preferred spices
2–3 tbsp. olive oil
various dips such as ajvar
    or guacamole

1. Preheat the oven to 200°C (400°F).

2. Wash and dry the potatoes.

3. Place each potato on a spoon and make slits all the way along (without cutting all the way through), leaving only a narrow gap in between each slit.

4. Transfer the potatoes to a baking tray lined with baking paper and carefully press the slits apart.

5. Season the potatoes with your favourite spices and drizzle over some oil and bake for around 40–50 minutes until golden brown and crispy.

6. Serve the hasselback potatoes with dips.

Avocado toast with garlic mushrooms

20 mins
Makes 2

200 g (1⅔ cups) mushrooms
½ onion (optional)
1 large garlic clove
1–2 tbsp. olive oil
1–2 tbsp. soy sauce or tamari
2 slices of bread

For the guacamole:
1 avocado
1 tsp. lemon juice
salt
pepper
a little coconut milk
a handful of fresh basil

For the topping (optional):
sesame seeds
fresh herbs

1. Clean and slice the mushrooms. Peel and finely chop the onion and garlic.

2. Heat the olive oil in a large frying pan and fry the mushrooms for around 5 minutes until golden brown on each side.

3. Add the onion and garlic and continue to fry for a further 1–2 minutes. Douse with the soy sauce and fry on a low heat for a further 1–2 minutes.

4. Halve the avocado, remove the stone and scoop out the flesh with a spoon. Using a stick blender, purée all the ingredients for the guacamole until creamy (or simply mash with a fork). Season to taste with salt and pepper.

5. Toast the bread.

6. Spread the guacamole over the toast and place the fried mushrooms on top.

7. Add a little more salt and pepper and sprinkle with fresh herbs and sesame seeds (or other toppings).

Spinach wraps with cashew cheese

20 mins + 4 hours soaking time
Makes 3

350 g (10 cups) fresh spinach
salt
1 red pepper
1 red onion
1 garlic clove
1–2 tbsp. lemon juice
freshly milled pepper
3 tortilla wraps, ready-made

For the cashew cheese:
200 g (1⅓ cups) cashew nuts
1–2 tbsp. lemon juice
2 tbsp. nutritional yeast flakes
1–2 tbsp. plant-based yoghurt,
   as required
1 small garlic clove

1. Soak the cashew nuts for at least 4 hours (or preferably overnight).

2. Strain the soaked cashew nuts through a sieve and rinse with cold water. Transfer to a food processor or blender along with the lemon juice, salt, yeast flakes, garlic and, if needed, a little vegan yoghurt and blend to a creamy purée. Set aside.

3. Bring a large pan of salted water to the boil. Remove the lid and cook the spinach in boiling water for about a minute until it's light green. Then plunge it into a bowl of iced water (this interrupts the cooking process and retains the vitamins).

4. Squeeze out any excess moisture and finely chop.

5. Wash, halve and finely dice the peppers.

6. Peel and finely chop the onion and garlic and stir into the cashew cheese. Season with lemon juice, salt and pepper. Mix in the spinach and diced pepper.

7. Briefly warm the tortillas in a dry frying pan.

8. Spread the cashew and spinach mixture over the top and roll up. Cut each tortilla in half and serve.

Savoury crêpes with spinach, guacamole and garlic mushrooms

25 mins
Makes 3–4 crêpes

160 g (1⅛ cups) chickpea flour
   or buckwheat flour
240 ml (1 cup) water
salt
pepper
300 g (2½ cups) mushrooms
3 garlic cloves
olive oil
1 avocado
a squeeze of lemon
a handful of baby spinach
4 tsp. pine nuts

1. Combine the chickpea flour with the water in a medium-sized bowl.

2. Season with salt and pepper and leave to stand for 10 minutes.

3. While you're waiting, brush a non-stick frying pan with a little oil and heat.

4. Pour a little batter into the pan and spread out evenly so that it coats the base of the pan. Fry for around 4 minutes, then carefully turn over and fry the other side until it's golden brown.

5. Repeat this with the rest of the batter.

6. Wash, clean and slice the mushrooms. Peel and finely chop the garlic. Heat a little olive oil in a frying pan and fry the mushrooms over a medium heat for a few minutes until softened and lightly browned. Add the garlic and fry for another 30 seconds.

7. Halve the avocado, remove the stone and mash the flesh with a fork. Mix in the lemon juice. Season with salt and pepper. Wash and drain the spinach, and sauté for 1–2 minutes, or until wilted. Toast the pine nuts in a dry frying pan.

8. Fill the chickpea crêpes with the guacamole, spinach and mushrooms, and fold. Sprinkle with pine nuts. Enjoy!

Cakes

Marble cake

This vegan marble cake brings back memories of childhood.

1 hour + 1 hour to cool
Makes 1 cake

300 g (2⅓ cups) all-purpose
    or light spelt flour
    (see also page 13)
35 g (⅓ cup) cornflour
1 tbsp. soya flour
    (optional)
175 g (¾ cup) sugar
1 tbsp. baking powder
½ tsp. bicarbonate of soda
a pinch of salt
300 ml (1¼ cups) plant
    milk + approx. 5 tbsp.
160 ml (⅔ cup) mild-
    tasting oil, e.g. rapeseed
    or sunflower oil
1 tsp. vanilla extract
juice of half a lemon or
    1–2 tbsp. apple cider
    vinegar
zest of half an unwaxed
    orange
3 tbsp. cocoa powder
walnuts or other nuts
    to garnish

1. Preheat the oven to 180°C (350°F). Grease a loaf tin (approx. 23–25 cm/9–10 in. long) and dust with flour.

2. Mix the flour, cornflour, soya milk (if using), sugar, baking powder, bicarbonate of soda and salt in a large bowl.

3. Make a small well in the centre. Pour 300 ml (1¼ cups) plant milk into the well along with the oil, vanilla extract, lemon juice and orange zest and combine to form a smooth batter. (Do not over-mix or else the cake won't rise.)

4. Transfer half the batter into another large bowl. Add the cocoa powder to the original bowl along with around 5 tablespoons of plant milk and mix well.

5. Layer the two batters into the tin. To create a marble effect, use a separate spoon for each batter. First place a large spoonful of the vanilla batter into the centre of the cake tin, then place a large spoonful of the chocolate batter into the centre of the vanilla batter. Continue to spoon the batter into the centre in alternate layers until it's all gone. (The mixture will spread itself out in the tin to create the marble effect. To help it along, give the tin a little shake now and then.)

Continued on the
next page ▶

For the ganache:
100 g (⅔ cup) vegan dark
   chocolate, chopped
3 tbsp. plant milk

6. Bake the cake for around 50 minutes (or until a skewer comes out clean).

7. Leave the cake to cool in the tin for about an hour, then turn it out onto a cooling rack to cool completely.

8. To make the ganache, slowly melt the chocolate in a bowl over a pan of boiling water, stirring occasionally. Once it's melted, add the plant milk and mix well to give the mixture a smooth and creamy consistency.

9. Pour the ganache over the cooled cake and use a brush to spread it out evenly.

10. Decorate the cake with chopped walnuts or other nuts of your choice.

Chocolate peanut butter cake

A fantastic cake inspired by the well-known peanut chocolate bar.
It's moist, creamy and simply delicious!

1½ hours + 4 hours to cool
Makes 1 cake

320 ml (1⅓ cups) plant milk
1 tbsp. apple cider vinegar
320 g (2½ cups) flour
1 tbsp. soya flour
270 g (1¼ cups) raw cane sugar
65 g (½ cup) cocoa powder
2 tsp. baking powder
1 tsp. bicarbonate of soda
a pinch of salt
160 ml (⅔ cup) coconut oil,
   melted
180 g (¾ cup) unsweetened
   apple purée
1 tbsp. vanilla extract
120 ml (½ cup) strong coffee
   or more milk
salted peanuts to decorate
   (optional)

For the icing:
450 g (2 cups) vegan cream
   cheese (at room temperature)
8 tbsp. smooth peanut butter,
   melted
1 tsp. vanilla extract
100 g (⅔ cup) icing sugar

Continued on the
next page ▶

1. Preheat the oven to 175°C (350°F) and grease two springform tins (20 cm/8 in.). (To make it easier to remove the cake from the tin later, you could also line it with baking paper.)

2. Whisk together the plant milk and vinegar in a measuring jug. Place to one side so it thickens and turns into a sort of vegan buttermilk.

3. Sieve the flour, soya flour, sugar, cocoa powder, baking powder, bicarbonate of soda and salt into a large bowl and mix.

4. Add the coconut oil, apple purée, vanilla extract and vegan buttermilk. Mix with a hand mixer on the medium setting until everything is well combined. Reduce the speed a little, pour in the coffee and mix. (You can also add a little sugar if you like.)

5. Divide the mixture evenly between the two springform tins. Bake for around 30 minutes until a skewer comes out mostly clean. (Don't bake for too long, else the cake will dry out.)

6. Once baked, leave the cake in the tin to cool for approx. 10 minutes, then turn it out and leave to cool completely before adding the icing.

7. To make the icing, blend the cream cheese with a hand mixer until smooth. Stir in the peanut butter and vanilla extract. Sieve in the icing sugar and blend until creamy. (If the icing is too thick to spread, add a little plant milk. If it's too runny, add more icing sugar.)

For the ganache:

125 g (¾ cup) vegan dark
    chocolate, chopped
4 tbsp. plant milk or soya cream

8. Slice each of the cooled cakes horizontally into two evenly-sized layers.

9. Place one layer onto a serving plate. Spread about a quarter of the icing on top and lay the next layer of cake on top. Repeat this process with the next two layers. After the fourth layer, use the rest of the icing to cover the whole cake, including the sides. (You can also keep a small portion of the peanut butter icing to one side for decorating using a piping bag.) Leave the cake to stand in the fridge for at least 4 hours (or preferably overnight).

10. To make the ganache, slowly melt the chocolate in a heat-proof bowl over a pan of boiling water (or in the microwave), stirring occasionally. Gradually stir in the milk until the ganache is smooth and creamy.

11. Using a teaspoon, carefully spread the ganache around the outer edge of the cake, allowing it to drip down the sides slightly. Spread the rest over the top of the cake.

12. Place the cake into the fridge for around 5 minutes to allow the chocolate to set.

13. You can now pipe little swirls of the leftover peanut icing onto the cake and decorate with peanuts.

Lemon and poppy seed cake

1 hour + 15 mins to cool
Makes 1 cake

240 ml (1 cup) plant milk
1 unwaxed lemon,
 zest and juice
300 g (2⅓ cups) all-purpose
 or light spelt flour
 (see also page 13)
1 tbsp. baking powder
1 tsp. bicarbonate of soda
½ tsp. salt
150 g (⅔ cup) sugar
125 ml (½ cup) coconut oil
1 tsp. vanilla extract
3–4 tbsp. poppy seeds

For the icing:
200 g (1 cup) vegan cream
 cheese
60 g (½ cup) icing sugar
1–2 tbsp. lemon juice
⅓ tsp. vanilla extract

Continued on the
next page ▶

1. Preheat the oven to 180°C (350°F). Grease a loaf tin (approx. 23–25 cm/9–10 in. long) and line with baking paper. (If necessary, trim any excess paper.) You can also bake the cake in a tray measuring approx. 23 × 23 cm/9 in. × 9 in. (In that case, the baking time is reduced to approx. 20 minutes.)

2. Combine the plant milk and lemon juice in a measuring jug and leave it to curdle until it forms a sort of vegan buttermilk.

3. Sieve the flour, baking powder, bicarbonate of soda and salt into a large bowl. Add the sugar and combine all the dry ingredients with a whisk.

4. Make a well in the centre of the flour mixture and add the vegan buttermilk, oil, vanilla extract, lemon zest and poppy seeds. Mix until everything is combined. (But not for too long, else the cake won't be light and fluffy.)

5. Pour the batter into the loaf tin and smooth over the top. (Tap the tin on the work surface a few times to knock out any bubbles in the batter.)

For the topping:

flaked almonds
1 tbsp. brown sugar
1 unwaxed lemon, sliced
   (optional)

6. Bake the cake for an initial 15 minutes. Then make a cut down the middle and bake for a further 35–45 minutes or until a skewer placed into the centre comes out clean. (If the cake starts to get too dark while baking, cover it with a piece of foil or baking paper.)

7. Once baked, leave the cake to cool in the tin for 10–15 minutes. Turn it out onto a cooling rack and allow to cool completely.

8. To make the icing, place the vegan cream cheese, icing sugar, lemon juice and vanilla extract into a tall mixing jug and blend until smooth and creamy.

9. Evenly spread the icing over the cooled cake.

10. Toast the flaked almonds in a large frying pan over a medium heat. Sprinkle over the brown sugar and caramelise. Once the almonds are lightly browned, remove from the pan.

11. Sprinkle the toasted almonds over the icing and decorate with lemon slices.

Blackberry tart

This delicious tart is really quick to make and doesn't require any baking.
The perfect cake for summer!

50 mins + 4 hours to freeze
Makes 1 tart

85 g (⅜ cup) vegan butter
28 Oreo cookies (320 g/11
   oz) or other biscuits with a
   creamy filling
225 g (1¼ cups) blackberries
   and blueberries + a few more
   for decoration
225 g (1 cup) vegan cream
   cheese or soya quark
75 g (½ cup) sugar
2 tsp. vanilla extract
240 ml (1 cup) plant-based
   whipping cream, chilled
60 ml (¼ cup) plant milk
1 tsp. 100% agar powder

1. Melt the butter in a small saucepan. Place the whole Oreo cookies (including the filling) into a food processor and blend to fine crumbs. Transfer the crumbs to a bowl, add the butter and mix well.

2. Cover the base and sides of a tart tin (23 cm/9 in.) – or another tin with a removable base – with the biscuit mixture and press down well. Chill for 15 minutes in the freezer (or 30 minutes in the fridge) until the base is firm.

3. Place the blackberries and blueberries into a blender and purée until smooth (or use a stick blender). Add the vegan cream cheese, sugar and vanilla extract and blend until smooth. Set aside.

4. Using a hand mixer, beat the vegan whipping cream until it forms stiff peaks. Place in the fridge to use later.

5. Stir the agar into the plant milk in a small saucepan and cook for approx. 2 minutes (or as per the packet instructions). Remove from the heat and allow to cool, stirring occasionally.

Continued on the
next page ▶

6. Carefully stir the agar mixture into the berry purée and fold in the whipped cream. (Only stir for as long as it takes to ensure everything is thoroughly combined.) Spoon the berry mousse mixture into the tart tin with the biscuit base and smooth over the top. Chill the tart in the fridge for at least 4 hours (or preferably overnight) until it has set.

7. Once the mousse has set, remove the tart from the tin by carefully pushing up the base of the tin from underneath. Garnish with berries or other decorations. Serve chilled.

TOP TIP:

If you'd like the biscuit base to be crispier, bake it in the oven at 180°C (350°F) for 5–6 minutes. Allow to cool completely before adding the mousse filling, otherwise the mousse will melt.

If you are unable to get hold of vegan whipping cream, you can use coconut milk instead. Chill 1–2 tins overnight in the fridge. The next day, scoop out the solid part from the top of the tin. You can use the watery part for something else.

Chocolate and banana bread

This banana bread is one of my favourite recipes.
It's unbelievably light, moist and tasty!

1 hour
Makes 1 loaf

160 g (1¼ cups) all-purpose or
   spelt flour (see also page 13)
1 tbsp. cornflour
50 g (½ cup) cocoa powder
1 tsp. baking powder
1 tsp. bicarbonate of soda
½ tsp. salt
2 large, very ripe bananas
100 ml (½ cup) plant milk
75 g (⅓ cup) coconut oil
115 g (½ cup) sugar
1 tsp. vanilla extract
1 tsp. apple cider vinegar
chocolate chips (optional)

1. Preheat the oven to 175°C (350°F). Grease a loaf tin (25 cm/10 in.) and line with baking paper (the grease helps the paper stick to the tin).

2. Whisk together the flour, cornflour, cocoa powder, baking powder, bicarbonate of soda and salt in a bowl.

3. Mash the bananas with a fork and transfer to a measuring jug. Add the plant milk, oil, sugar, vanilla extract and apple cider vinegar and mix well.

4. Pour this mixture into a bowl, add the flour mixture and mix until well combined.

5. Spoon the batter into the loaf tin and, if using, sprinkle over the chocolate chips. Bake the banana bread for around 40–50 minutes until a skewer comes out mostly clean.
(If you want the banana bread to be moist, make sure not to bake it for too long.)

6. Allow to cool in the tin. Using the baking paper to help you, carefully remove the cake from the tin.

7. Cut the chocolate and banana bread into slices and enjoy!

Carrot cake

Carrot cake is a real classic and this delicious recipe will make
you want to bake it time and time again!

1½ hours
Makes 1 cake

2–3 large carrots
125 g (1 cup) vegan butter
   (at room temperature)
100 g (½ cup) sugar
a pinch of salt
a dash of vanilla extract
2 portions of egg substitute,
   e.g. flax seeds
125 g (1 cup) flour
½ tsp. cinnamon
1½ tsp. baking powder
100 g (⅔ cup) ground almonds
1 tsp. apple cider vinegar
½ tsp. bicarbonate of soda

For the cream filling:
200 g (1 cup) vegan
   cream cheese
80 g (½ cup) icing sugar
a squeeze of lemon
a dash of vanilla extract

For the topping:
marzipan carrots
chopped pistachios

1. Brush a springform tin (20 cm/8 in.) with butter or oil.
Preheat the oven to 180°C (350°F).

2. To make the batter, peel and finely grate the carrots.
In a mixing bowl, cream together the butter, sugar, salt
and vanilla extract.

3. Gradually stir in the egg substitute. Add the carrots
and give it a quick stir.

4. Sieve in the flour, cinnamon and baking powder.

5. Add the almonds, bicarbonate of soda and vinegar.
Give everything a quick stir.

6. Transfer the batter to the cake tin, smooth over the
top and bake in the centre of the oven for 35–40 minutes.
(Don't forget to test it using a skewer!)

7. Once baked, turn the cake out onto a cooling rack and
leave to cool for 10 minutes. Remove from the tin and allow
to cool completely.

8. Using a hand mixer with the whisk attachments, mix all the
ingredients for the creamy icing to a smooth consistency and
spread over the cake using a spatula or spoon.

9. Decorate with marzipan carrots and pistachios.

10. Chill the cake in the fridge until you're ready to serve it.
(It will stay nice and moist for 3–4 days.)

Blueberry crumble cheesecake

1 hour 10 mins + 30 mins to cool
Makes 1 cake

200 g (1½ cups) all-purpose or
  spelt flour (see also page 13)
50 g (⅓ cup) ground almonds
½ tbsp. baking powder
100 g (½ cup) raw cane sugar
½ tsp. cinnamon
a pinch of salt
150 g (⅔ cup) soft vegan butter
50 g (¼ cup) unsweetened apple
  purée
zest of half a lemon
soya milk, if required

For the filling:
25 g (⅛ cup) vegan butter
250 g (½ cup) soya quark
3 tbsp. coconut milk
juice of half a lemon
3 tbsp. raw cane sugar
2½ tbsp. cornflour
½ tsp. vanilla extract
250 g (1⅓ cups) blueberries

TOP TIP:
If the cheesecake starts to get too dark while baking, simply cover the top with a piece of baking paper or foil.

1. Combine the flour with the ground almonds, baking powder, sugar, cinnamon and a pinch of salt. Cut the butter into small cubes and add to the flour mixture. Add the apple purée and lemon zest and knead to form a crumbly dough using a hand mixer with the dough hook attachment. Using your hands, knead to form a smooth dough. (If the dough is too dry, add a little cold soya milk.)

2. Shape the dough into a ball, wrap in cling film and place in the fridge to chill for at least half an hour to make it easier to work with.

3. Remove the dough from the fridge. Spread two thirds of the dough evenly over a greased springform tin (18 cm/7½ in.) and press down well.

4. Preheat the oven to 175°C (350°F).

5. To make the filling, slowly melt the vegan butter in a small saucepan and set aside to cool a little.

6. Place the quark, coconut milk, sugar, cornflour, and vanilla extract into a mixing bowl and blend with a hand mixer until creamy. Mix in the softened butter and lemon juice. Carefully fold in two thirds of the blueberries.

7. Spread the filling onto the dough base and smooth over the top.

8. Crumble up the rest of the dough and sprinkle on top of the filling along with the blueberries.

9. Bake the cheesecake in the centre of the pre-heated oven at 175°C (350°F) for around an hour.

10. Leave the cheesecake to cool before serving.

Black Forest gateau

This is my favourite recipe ever! It's simply divine.

40 mins + 1 hour to cool
Makes 1 cake

175 g (1⅓ cups) flour
3 tbsp. cornflour
100 g (½ cup) sugar
2 tbsp. cocoa powder
1 tsp. baking powder
a pinch of salt
60 ml (¼ cup) plant oil
   (mild-tasting)
200 ml (¾ cup) mineral
   water or plant milk
2 tsp. apple cider vinegar
½ tsp. bicarbonate of soda
3–4 tbsp. vegan chocolate,
   grated, to decorate

For the cherry compote:
350 g (1¾ cups) cherries
   (from a jar or tin)
230 ml (1 cup) cherry juice
50 g (¼ cup) sugar
30 g (¼ cup) cornflour

For the cream filling:
500 ml (2 cups) vegan
   cream
1 tsp. cream of tartar
½ tsp. Bourbon vanilla
   extract

1. Preheat the oven to 180°C (160°C fan) [350°F or 325°F fan] and line the base of a springform cake tin (18 cm/7½ in.) with baking paper.

2. Combine the flour, cornflour, sugar, cocoa powder, baking powder and salt in a bowl. Add the oil and water and then the apple cider vinegar and bicarbonate of soda. Whisk to form a smooth batter. Transfer the batter to the cake tin and bake for approx. 25 minutes until a skewer comes out clean. Leave to cool completely. Cut into three evenly-sized layers.

3. Drain the cherries and collect the juice. Set seven cherries aside for decoration. Take around 2 tbsp. of the cherry juice and mix it with the sugar and cornflour in a small container. Transfer the rest of the cherry juice to a saucepan, bring to the boil and whisk in the cornflour mixture. Bring back to the boil and simmer briefly, stirring continuously. Remove from the heat and keep stirring as it cools. Carefully fold in the cherries.

4. Using a hand mixer on a high setting, beat the cream for approx. 1 minute, add the cream of tartar and continue to beat until it forms soft peaks. Chill in the fridge for at least an hour.

5. Spread half the cherry compote evenly over the bottom layer, leaving a gap of 1–2 cm (¼–¾ in.) around the edge. Spread a thin layer of cream on top, and then add the second layer of sponge. Spread the rest of the cherry compote on top of this and top with more of the cream. Place the third sponge layer on top and cover the whole gateau with cream, including the sides. Transfer a little of the cream to a piping bag and pipe seven little swirls on the top of the gateau. Place a cherry on top of each swirl and sprinkle the gateau with grated chocolate.

6. Chill in the fridge for at least an hour before serving.

Chocolate and raspberry gateau

This cake is perfect for special occasions and
certain to wow your guests.

I hour + 2 hours to cool
Makes I cake

1½ tbsp. apple cider
  vinegar
480 ml (2 cups) plant milk
225 g (I cup) vegan butter
1–2 tsp. instant coffee
  or espresso granules
2 tsp. vanilla extract
420 g (3⅛ cups) flour
65 g (½ cup) cocoa
  powder
250 g (1¼ cups) sugar
4 tsp. baking powder
1½ tsp. bicarbonate of soda
¾ tsp. salt
120 g (½ cup) apple purée
  or I puréed banana

For the icing:
300 ml (1¼ cups) vegan
  whipping cream or
  coconut milk
340 g (2 cups) vegan
  chocolate (60% cocoa),
  chopped
40 g (¼ cup) icing sugar

1. To make the icing, bring the cream to the boil in a
small saucepan (or heat in the microwave for approx.
2 minutes).

2. Place the chocolate in a bowl. Pour the hot cream
over the chocolate and stir until the chocolate
has melted.

3. Add the icing sugar and mix with a hand mixer
until smooth. Set aside 80 ml (⅓ cup) of this mixture
for the chocolate mousse.

4. Chill the rest of the mixture for 2 hours in the
fridge until it thickens to form a spreadable icing.

5. Using a hand mixer, blend together all the mousse
ingredients until creamy. Add the 80 ml (⅓ cup)
of chocolate cream and continue to whisk until it's
nice and creamy. (If the chocolate cream has set too
much in the meantime, you can always warm it up a
little to make it runny again.)

6. To make the raspberry jam, defrost the frozen
raspberries in a small saucepan over a medium heat,
stirring occasionally. Crush the raspberries with
a spoon.

7. In a small cup, dissolve the cornflour into 2 tbsp.
water. Stir into the raspberries along with the
sugar and lemon juice. Bring the mixture to the
boil, stirring continuously, and allow to simmer for
approx. 1–2 minutes until it thickens. Leave to cool.
(It will thicken as it cools.)

Continued on the
next page ▶

For the mousse:

60 g (¼ cup) vegan cream cheese or silken tofu, puréed
120 ml (½ cup) plant-based whipping cream or full-fat coconut milk
3 tbsp. icing sugar
½ tsp. vanilla extract

For the raspberry jam:

230 g (1¾ cups) frozen raspberries
2 tsp. cornflour
1 tbsp. sugar
a squeeze of lemon

For the topping:

raspberries
strawberries
vegan chocolate, chopped

8. Preheat the oven to 175°C (350°F). Grease three springform tins (20 cm/8 in.) and line with baking paper.

9. Mix the apple cider vinegar with the milk and leave to stand until it curdles to form a sort of vegan buttermilk.

10. In a small saucepan, slowly melt the vegan butter over a medium heat. Stir in the instant coffee and vanilla extract. Set aside to cool.

11. Combine the flour, cocoa powder, sugar, baking powder, bicarbonate of soda and salt in a bowl.

12. Pour the vegan buttermilk and melted butter mixture over the flour mixture. Add the apple purée and mix the batter to get rid of any large lumps (but don't over-mix). Add the sugar, depending how sweet a tooth you have.

13. Pour the batter into the tins and bake for around 30 minutes or until a skewer placed into the centre comes out mostly clean. (The longer you bake the cake for, the drier it will be. So don't bake for too long if you like it moist.) Leave to cool completely.

14. Remove the icing from the fridge and mix until creamy.

15. Place one layer of the cake onto a serving plate. Spread half the raspberry jam over the cake. Spread half the chocolate mousse over that. Place the second layer on top and repeat. Once you have placed the third layer on top, cover the whole gateau with the icing, including the sides.

16. Decorate the gateau with berries and chocolate.

Molehill cake

My molehill cake is covered with a delicious creamy chocolate ganache and filled with stracciatella-style cream, bananas and cherries. An irresistible combination!

50 mins + 2 hours to freeze
Makes 1 cake

100 g (½ cup) vegan margarine or vegan butter
90 g (½ cup) sugar
125 g (½ cup) mashed banana or apple purée
1½ tsp. baking powder
1 tsp. apple cider vinegar
240 g (2 cups) flour
1 tbsp. cornflour
½ tsp. vanilla extract
2 tbsp. unsweetened cocoa powder
a pinch of salt
150 ml (⅔ cup) plant milk

For the filling:

450 g (2 cups) vegan whipping cream
1 tsp. cream of tartar
2 tbsp. icing sugar
a dash of vanilla extract
75 g (½ cup) vegan chocolate, grated
2 bananas
150 g (1 cup) cherry compote

1. Preheat the oven to 180°C (350°F) and grease a round cake tin (20 cm/8 in.).

2. Using an electric hand mixer, cream together the soft margarine, sugar and banana purée.

3. In a small cup, combine the baking powder and apple cider vinegar and set aside.

4. Combine the flour, cornflour, cocoa powder, vanilla extract and salt in a mixing bowl. Add the banana mixture, then gradually add the plant milk, and the baking powder and vinegar mixture. Mix everything to form a smooth batter (if needed, add a little more milk).

5. Pour the batter into the greased tin and bake for around 35 minutes (or until a skewer placed into the centre comes out mostly clean). Leave the cake to cool.

6. Once cooled, carefully scoop out the middle of the cake, leaving a 1.5 cm (½ in.) rim and a 1 cm (⅓ in.) base. (To get an even rim, you may wish to mark out the inner circle with a sharp knife beforehand.)

7. Place the scooped-out cake in a bowl and crumble with your fingers. (We'll use these crumbs later for the topping.)

Continued on the next page ▶

8. Beat the vegan whipping cream for approx.
I minute using an electric hand mixer on a high
setting. Add the icing sugar, cream of tartar and
vanilla extract and continue to beat until the
mixture forms stiff peaks. Carefully fold in the grated
chocolate and place in the fridge to use later.

9. Peel the bananas, halve them lengthways and
place them onto the base of the cake. Spread the
cherry compote over the top.

10. Spoon over the whipped cream, piling it into
a sort of mound. Sprinkle the cake crumbs over
the cream and gently press them in. The cake
should now look like a mole hill!

II. Before serving, chill the cake in the fridge
for approx. 2 hours.

Chocolate mug cake

I love mug cakes! They're so easy to make – perfect for those times when you need a quick cake fix.

10 mins
Makes 1 mug cake

1 small mashed banana
2½ tbsp. plant milk
  of your choice
1 tbsp. nut butter
50 g (⅓ cup) flour
1 tbsp. cocoa powder
½ tsp. baking powder
1 tbsp. sugar
a pinch of vanilla extract
coconut oil for greasing

For the topping (as preferred):
chocolate sauce
granola
berries

1. Mix the banana with the milk, nut butter and vanilla extract.

2. Mix the flour with the cocoa powder, baking powder and sugar and add to the banana mixture.

3. Mix well to form a thick, smooth batter.

4. Grease a microwavable mug with coconut oil and fill with the batter.

5. Bake the mug cake for approx. 3 minutes in the microwave.

6. Add your favourite toppings and enjoy!

Best vegan cheesecake

The famous German baked cheesecake is rich, creamy and irresistibly tasty. While the traditional New York Cheesecake is made with heavy cream, eggs and cream cheese, I made this classic German version a little healthier with fresh strawberries on top. It is not only delicious, but also 100% vegan!

1 hour + 10 mins + time to cool (overnight)
Makes 1 cake with 12 slices

For the crust:
210 g (1⅔ cups) all-purpose or light spelt flour (see also page 13)
70 g (⅓ cup) sugar
140 g (½ cup) soft vegan butter

For the cheesecake mixture:
500 g (1 cup) soya quark
120 g (½ cup) vegan cream cheese
200 ml (¾ cup) vegan cream or full-fat coconut milk
120 g (½ cup) melted vegan butter
135 g (⅔ cup) sugar
50 g (½ cup) cornflour
1 tsp. vanilla extract
1 unwaxed lemon, juice & a little of the zest

For the topping:
½ tsp. 100% agar powder
200 ml (1 cup) red fruit juice
1–2 tsp. sugar (optional to taste)
500 g (2½ cups) strawberries

1. Preheat the oven to 180°C (350°F). Grease a springform tin (20–22 cm/8–9 in.) and line the base with baking paper.

2. Place the flour and sugar in a bowl. Cut the butter into cubes and add to the bowl, kneading with your hands to form a dough. Shape the dough into a ball, flatten slightly and wrap in cling film. Chill in the fridge for around half an hour.

3. Once chilled, place the dough between two sheets of cling film (or onto a lightly floured work surface) and roll into a large circle. Transfer to the tin and press down well onto the base and sides.

4. Prick the base a few times with a fork so that it doesn't rise while baking.

5. Place all the ingredients for the cheesecake filling into a mixing bowl and mix to a creamy consistency using an electric hand mixer.

6. Spoon the cheesecake mixture into the tin. Tap the cake tin on the worktop a few times to knock out any bubbles in the dough. This will stop the cheesecake cracking in the oven.

7. Bake the cheesecake for approx. 1 hour. Turn off the oven and open the oven door slightly. Leave the cheesecake in the oven for another 10 minutes. Then remove and leave to cool completely. For the best results, leave the cheesecake in the fridge overnight so that it can fully set.

8. In a small saucepan, stir the agar into the red fruit juice (+ sugar to taste) and bring to the boil. Cook for 1–2 minutes (or follow the package instructions). Set aside to cool a little.

9. Halve the strawberries and arrange on top of the chilled cheesecake. Using a tablespoon, drizzle the glaze over the top. Return to the fridge until the glaze has set.

Cherry pie

Cherry pie is an American classic. And rightly so—it's easy to make, only requires a few ingredients and tastes absolutely amazing.

50 mins
Makes 1 small pie

150 g (1¼ cups) all-purpose
  or light spelt flour
  (see also page 13)
½ tsp. baking powder
50 g (¼ cup) raw cane sugar
a pinch of vanilla extract
a pinch of salt
50 g (¼ cup) apple purée
90 g (⅜ cup) vegan butter or
  margarine
vegan cream or milk for brushing
icing sugar for dusting (optional)

For the filling:
350 g (1¾ cups) cherries, pitted
  (from a jar or tin)
200 ml (1 cup) cherry juice
3 tbsp. cornflour
2 tbsp. raw cane sugar

TOP TIP:
The pie tastes even better
the day after baking.

1. Combine the flour, baking powder, sugar and salt. Add the vanilla extract and apple purée. Cut the butter into small cubes and crumble into the flour mixture before quickly kneading everything into a smooth dough. (If the dough is too dry, add a little cold plant milk.) Shape the dough into a ball, wrap in cling film and place in the fridge to chill for at least 30 minutes.

2. Remove the dough from the fridge. On a floured work surface, roll out half the dough and line a greased springform tin (18 cm/7½ in.). Press the dough down into the tin, pulling it up 2–3 cm (¾–1 in.) around the sides.

3. Blind-bake the pastry case in an oven preheated to 180°C (350°F) for 15–20 minutes.

4. To make the filling, drain the cherries and save the juice.

5. In a small saucepan, mix the cherry juice together with the cornflour and sugar and bring to the boil. Stir in the cherries (if using fresh cherries, simmer for approx. 5 minutes) and leave to cool. Pour the filling into the pre-baked pastry case and smooth over the top.

6. Roll out the rest of the dough and cut it into 1 cm (⅓ in.)-wide strips. Arrange the strips on top of the pie in a criss-cross pattern to create a lattice, and trim off any excess pastry from the edges. Brush the pastry lattice with a little vegan cream or milk.

7. Bake the pie in the centre of the oven for around 20 minutes until golden.

8. Leave the pie to cool and then chill in the fridge until you're ready to serve.

9. Before serving, sprinkle the pie with a little icing sugar and serve with vanilla ice cream or coconut cream.

Brownies

These brownies are the best I've ever eaten! A chocolate lover's dream – you absolutely have to try them!

35 mins
Makes 8

2 tbsp. ground flax seeds
6 tbsp. hot water
175 g (¾ cup) vegan butter or coconut oil + more for greasing
250 g (1¼ cups) sugar
1 tsp. vanilla extract
150 g (1¼ cups) all-purpose or light spelt flour (see also page 13)
75 g (⅔ cup) unsweetened cocoa powder
1 tsp. baking powder
½ tsp. salt
approx. 80 ml (⅓ cup) plant milk
vegan chocolate drops (as many as you like)

1. Mix the flax seeds with the hot water and leave to soak for approx. 5 minutes.

2. Preheat the oven to 175°C (350°F). Grease a brownie tin (approx. 28 × 18 cm/11 × 7½ in.) with a little vegan butter and line with baking paper. (Greasing the tin will make the baking paper stick better.)

3. Slowly melt the vegan butter in a saucepan. Add the sugar and vanilla extract and stir well.

4. Sieve the flour, cocoa, baking powder and salt into a large bowl and mix together. Pour in the melted butter mixture, plant milk and flax seeds and combine to form a smooth batter (make sure you don't over-mix). Stir in half the chocolate drops.

5. Pour the batter into the brownie tin and smooth over the top. Sprinkle with the rest of the chocolate drops and bake for approx. 30 minutes or until the brownies have reached the desired consistency. (The longer you bake the brownies for, the drier they will be. If you like them nice and gooey, bake for less time.)

6. Leave the brownies to cool for 15 minutes. Using the baking paper to help you, remove from the tin and cool for a further 10 minutes.

7. Cut into individual brownies and enjoy!

Strawberries and cream layer cake

I love baking this wonderfully light and creamy cake for summer birthdays,
especially during strawberry season.

1 hour + 2 hours to cool
Makes 1 cake

220 g (1⅔ cups) all-purpose or light
   spelt flour (see also page 13)
1 tbsp. cornflour
1 tbsp. baking powder
½ tsp. bicarbonate of soda
a pinch of salt
130 g (⅔ cup) sugar
80 ml (⅓ cup) coconut oil
220 ml (1 cup) mineral water or
   plant milk
1 tsp. vanilla extract
zest of 1 lemon
1 tbsp. apple cider vinegar

For the cream filling:
250 ml (1 cup) vegan whipping
   cream
350 g (1½ cups) vegan mascarpone
   (or vegan cream cheese)
60 g (½ cup) icing sugar
1 vanilla pod
200 g (1 cup) strawberries
1 tbsp. icing sugar
1–2 tbsp. lemon juice

1. Preheat the oven to 180°C (350°F) and grease a
springform tin (20 cm/8 in.). (You could also line the tin with
baking paper to make the cake easier to remove from the tin.)

2. Sieve the flour, cornflour, baking powder and bicarbonate
of soda into a large bowl. Add the salt and sugar and mix well
with a whisk.

3. Add the oil, mineral water, vanilla extract, lemon zest and
vinegar. Give everything a quick stir so that all the ingredients
are combined. (Avoid mixing for too long or the cake won't
be light and fluffy. Don't worry if the batter has a few lumps
in it, as these will dissolve while it's baking.)

4. Transfer the batter to the tin and bake for approx.
35 minutes or until a skewer stuck into the middle comes
out clean and the top of the cake springs back when you
press it with your finger.

5. Remove the cake from the oven and leave to cool in the
tin for 15 minutes. Carefully turn it out onto a cooling rack
and allow to cool completely.

6. Using a stick blender (or food processor), blend the
strawberries, icing sugar and lemon juice to a purée.
Place in the fridge.

Continued on the
next page ▶

For the topping:
300 g (1½ cups) strawberries,
   sliced
50 g (⅓ cup) vegan white
   chocolate, grated

7. Cut along the length of the vanilla pod and scrape out the seeds. Cream the mascarpone, icing sugar and vanilla using a hand mixer and set aside.

8. In a separate mixing jug, beat the vegan whipping cream until it forms stiff peaks. Carefully fold in the mascarpone mixture.

9. Slice the cake horizontally into three evenly-sized layers. Place one layer of sponge onto a serving plate and, if you want to make it extra neat, place a cake ring on top.

10. Cover with a third of the strawberry mixture. Top with a quarter of the vanilla cream. Place the next layer of sponge on top and add another third of the strawberry mixture, followed by a quarter of the vanilla cream. Repeat this process for the third layer.

11. Carefully remove the cake ring (if used) and use the rest of the vanilla cream to cover the whole cake, including the sides.

12. Leave the cake to stand in the fridge for at least an hour before decorating and serving.

13. Decorate the cake with slices of strawberry and sprinkle with grated chocolate. Serve chilled and enjoy!

To make the cream featured in this photograph, simply whip 250 ml (1 cup) vegan whipping cream. Cream together 350 g (1½ cups) vegan mascarpone (or vegan cream cheese), 60 g (½ cup) icing sugar and a little vanilla and stir into the whipped cream.

Desserts

Cinnamon rolls

Is there anything nicer than the scent of freshly baked cinnamon buns in the morning? What makes this recipe so unique is that the glaze is made from a delicious cashew and coconut cream.

40 mins + 1 hour 10 mins
to prove + 20 mins to bake
Makes 12

2½ tbsp. fresh yeast
    (or 1 tbsp. dry yeast)
75 g (⅓ cup) coconut sugar
250 ml (1 cup) soya milk,
    lukewarm
75 g (⅜ cup) coconut oil
1 tbsp. cinnamon
¼ tsp. cardamom
1 tsp. salt
500 g (4 cups) all-purpose
    or light spelt flour
    (see also page 13)
2 tsp. vegan butter (optional)

For the filling:
50 g (¼ cup) vegan butter
1 tbsp. coconut sugar
2 tbsp. coconut syrup
2 tsp. cinnamon
60 g (½ cup) walnuts
50 g (⅓ cup) raisins

For the glaze:
75 g (½ cup) cashew nuts
    (soaked in water for approx.
    4 hours) or cashew butter
1 tbsp. coconut syrup
1 tbsp. coconut oil
50 g (⅓ cup) icing sugar
2–4 tbsp. plant milk

1. Crumble the yeast and dissolve in the warm soya milk (approx. 35°C/95°F) along with 1 tbsp. sugar.

2. Melt the coconut oil and add to the milk mixture. Stir in the remaining sugar, cinnamon, cardamom and salt. Add the flour and knead the dough with your hands for approx. 10 minutes. It should now be smooth and stretchy. Transfer the dough to a large bowl, cover with a damp tea towel and leave to prove in a warm place for 40 minutes.

3. While you're waiting, prepare the filling by melting the vegan butter over a low heat. Add the coconut sugar, coconut syrup and cinnamon and mix to form a syrupy consistency. If you're using nuts, chop them up and mix with the raisins.

4. Once the dough has doubled in size, transfer it to a floured work surface and roll it out into a large rectangle, around 1 cm (⅓ in.) thick. Spread the filling onto the dough.

5. Roll the dough up, starting from the longer side, and then cut into equally-sized pieces (approx. 3.5 cm/1⅓ in. wide). Place the cinnamon rolls into a greased tin, leaving plenty of space between each one. Cover again and prove for a further 30–45 minutes.

6. Preheat the oven to 180°C (350°F). For a more golden colour you can melt a little vegan butter to brush over the rolls. Bake for approx. 20 minutes.

7. Mix all the ingredients for the glaze in a high-powered blender to form a smooth and creamy sauce. If needed, thin it out with a little milk. (If you don't have a blender, you can use cashew butter and then all you have to do is stir in the other ingredients.)

8. Once baked, allow the cinnamon rolls to cool a little, drizzle with the glaze and serve.

Linzer cookies

Linzer cookies are not only a biscuit tin essential – this home-made version also makes a lovely gift for Valentine's Day!

30 mins + 1 hour to chill +
10 mins to bake
Makes approx. 15

300 g (2⅓ cups) all-purpose
  or light spelt flour
  (see also page 13)
50 g (⅓ cup) ground almonds
80 g (⅓ cup) caster sugar
a dash of Bourbon vanilla extract
a little unwaxed lemon zest
175 g (¾ cup) margarine or
  vegan butter
3 tbsp. almond milk
100 g (⅓ cup) jam, e.g.
  strawberry/raspberry
icing sugar for dusting

1. Mix together the flour, almonds, sugar and lemon zest.

2. Add the margarine, almond milk and vanilla extract and knead to form a smooth dough.

3. Shape the dough into a ball, wrap in cling film and place in the fridge to chill for about an hour.

4. Preheat the oven to 180°C (350°F).

5. Remove the dough from the fridge and roll out on a floured work surface to a thickness of approx. 3 mm/⅕ in.

6. Using a biscuit cutter or knife, cut into discs.

7. Using a small heart-shaped cutter, cut out hearts in the middle of half the discs.

8. Spread out the biscuits on a baking tray lined with baking paper and bake for approx. 10 minutes. Leave to cool.

9. Place the jam in a small saucepan to melt it. It will set again once it's cooled.

10. Using a pastry brush, spread some jam onto the bottom biscuit and sandwich together with the top biscuit. Then fill the little hearts with more jam.

11. Leave the biscuits to cool until the jam has set. Dust with icing sugar. Enjoy!

Cookie dough

Snaffling the dough is the best bit of baking cookies. That's why I came up with this delicious and healthy recipe that means you can snaffle the cookie dough without a guilty conscience!

15 mins
Makes 1 portion

1 tin (400 g/2 cups) chickpeas
2 tbsp. peanut butter
2 tbsp. maple syrup
  (or date syrup)
1 tsp. vanilla extract
approx. 2 tbsp. plant milk
2 tbsp. fine oats
60 g (⅓ cup) vegan chocolate
  drops

TOP TIP:
This cookie dough tastes amazing with creamy vegan caramel sauce. To make it, bring a glug of plant milk to the boil and stir in a few vegan toffees until they have melted.

If you prefer, you can replace the oats with the same quantity of protein powder.

1. Drain and rinse the chickpeas and shake off any excess water. Transfer the chickpeas, peanut butter, maple syrup, vanilla extract and milk to a blender (or use a stick blender) and purée to a creamy consistency.

2. Place the oats in a food processor and grind into flour. Add to the chickpea mixture and knead everything into a smooth dough. (If needed, add a little more milk or oat flour to achieve the desired consistency.)

3. Lastly, mix the chocolate drops into the dough.

4. You can either shape the chickpea cookie dough into little balls or spoon it straight from the jar.

Mousse au chocolat

25 mins + 3 hours to freeze
Makes 3 portions

120 g (¾ cup) vegan dark
   chocolate (70% cocoa)
a little plant milk, as required
240 ml (1 cup) aquafaba (water
   drained from tinned chickpeas)
½ tsp. vanilla extract (optional)
1–2 tbsp. sugar (optional)
coconut cream
1 tbsp. grated chocolate
   for decoration (optional)

TOP TIP:
One 400 g (2 cups) tin of
chickpeas contains 240 ml
(1 cup) aquafaba. You can
use the chickpeas for other
recipes such as chickpea
curry, falafel or hummus.

1. Break the chocolate into small pieces and place in a small microwavable dish.

2. Place the bowl over a pan of boiling water and slowly melt the chocolate.

3. Once the chocolate is melted, stir it up with a spoon or a small whisk. If required, add a little milk to improve the consistency. Remove from the heat and leave to cool.

4. Open a tin of chickpeas and drain the water into a large mixing jug. For extra flavour you can add some vanilla extract. (Ensure there are no traces of fat on the utensils, as this will make it difficult to whip the aquafaba.)

5. Using a hand mixer, beat the aquafaba for approx. 5 minutes until it's stiff and fluffy.

6. If you'd like the chocolate mousse to be sweeter, add a little sugar while beating.

7. Once the chocolate is cool, carefully fold into the aquafaba. (It's normal for the mixture to collapse a little at this stage.)

8. Divide the mousse into three glasses, giving it a little stir here and there.

9. Transfer the glasses to the fridge and chill for at least 3 hours (or preferably overnight), until the mousse has set.

10. Whip the coconut cream, spoon it on top of the mousse and sprinkle with a little chocolate or decorate with your preferred toppings.

Apple turnovers

30 mins
Makes 8

2 apples
75 ml (⅓ cup) water
1 tbsp. cornflour
1 tbsp. raw cane sugar +
   a little extra for sprinkling
1 tsp. cinnamon
a dash of vanilla extract
1 sheet of ready-rolled vegan
   puff pastry
vegan cream or vegan condensed
   milk for brushing

1. Wash the apples and cut into small chunks. Combine the water, cornflour, sugar, cinnamon and vanilla extract in a saucepan.

2. Bring to the boil, stirring continuously, then add the apples and set aside.

3. Place the pastry sheet onto a baking tray lined with baking paper. Cut into 8 squares and brush the edges with vegan condensed milk.

4. Spoon 1–2 tbsp. of the apple filling onto half of each square and fold over. Seal the edges using a fork.

5. Score each turnover three times to allow the heat to escape and brush the tops with either vegan cream or vegan condensed milk. Sprinkle with sugar and bake in an oven preheated to 220°C (425°F) for 10–15 minutes until the pastry has puffed up and turned golden brown.

Waffles

15 mins
Makes 4

1 ripe banana
approx. 90 ml (⅓ cup) plant milk
1 tbsp. melted vegan butter
  or coconut oil
1 tsp. agave syrup
90 g (¾ cup) spelt flour
1 tsp. baking powder
a splash of mineral water
a pinch of Bourbon vanilla extract
a pinch of cinnamon
coconut oil to grease the
  waffle iron

For the topping (as preferred):
peanut butter
vegan chocolate spread
banana
blueberries
blackberries

1. Purée the banana and cream together with the plant milk, vegan butter and syrup, to taste.

2. Combine the flour, baking powder and cinnamon and add to the banana mixture along with the vanilla extract and mineral water. Mix quickly to form a smooth, thick and creamy batter.

3. Preheat the waffle iron and brush with oil.

4. Pour the batter into the waffle iron and leave until the waffles are cooked.

5. Serve with your favourite toppings and enjoy!

Blueberry loaf

My vegan version of this yeast cake or 'Babka' is delicious and comforting.

1 hour + 1 hour 45 mins
to prove + 40 mins to bake
Makes 1 loaf

150 ml (⅔ cup) soya milk
2½ tbsp. fresh yeast
3 tbsp. coconut sugar
290 g (2⅓ cups) all-purpose
   or light spelt flour
   (see also page 13)
½ tsp. salt
70 g (⅓ cup) soft vegan
   butter
150 g (½ cup) blueberry
   jam
80 g (½ cup) icing sugar
2 tbsp. lemon juice

1. Heat the soya milk to between 37 and 45°C/100 and 110°F (lukewarm). Stir in the yeast and 1 tablespoon of the sugar. Set aside for 10 minutes until the mixture starts to froth.

2. In a large bowl, combine the flour with the salt and the rest of the sugar. Make a well in the centre and add the yeast mixture, along with the butter. Mix thoroughly with your hands and then knead the dough for approx. 8–10 minutes until it's smooth and stretchy.

3. Transfer the dough to a large greased bowl, cover with a tea towel (or cling film) and leave in a warm place to prove for approx. 1 hour, until it has doubled in size.

4. Turn the dough out onto a floured work surface and give it a quick knead to push out any air bubbles that may have formed. Roll the dough into a rectangle (approx. 30 x 40 cm/12 x 16 in.). Spread the jam over the top, leaving a 1.5 cm (½ in.) rim around the sides. Starting with the shorter side, roll the dough up to make a 30 cm (12 in.)-long roll. Using a sharp knife, slice it in half lengthways.

5. Gently press the upper ends of each strand together, then cross one half over the other and repeat to form a plait. Finally, gently press to lower ends together.

6. Carefully transfer the plait to a greased loaf tin (30 x 11 cm/ 12 x 4 in.). Again, cover with a tea towel (or cling film) and leave in a warm place to prove for a further 45 minutes.

7. Preheat the oven to 180°C (350°F) and bake the bread for approx. 40 minutes until golden. Once it's baked, remove from the oven and leave to cool in the tin for 10 minutes. Remove from the tin.

8. For the glaze, mix together icing sugar and lemon juice to form a smooth paste. Drizzle over the loaf and, for the best results, serve right away!

Strawberry ice cream

10 mins + 8 hours
to freeze
Makes 2 portions

180 ml (¾ cup) plant-
based whipping cream
240 ml (1 cup) coconut
cream
250 g (1¼ cups)
strawberries
90 g (⅓ cup) dates
1 tsp. vanilla extract

1. In a mixing bowl, beat the cold whipping cream with a hand mixer until it forms stiff peaks. Place in the fridge to use later.

2. Place the coconut cream, strawberries, dates and vanilla extract into a blender and mix until smooth.

3. Transfer to a large mixing bowl and carefully fold in the whipped cream. Only stir it for as long as it takes to mix everything together, otherwise the whipped cream will collapse.

4. Put the ice cream mixture straight in the freezer and leave overnight. If you have one, you can also use an ice cream maker. In this case, make the ice cream according to the instruction manual.

Grams to Cups Conversion Chart

Butter

Cups	Grams	Ounces
¼ cup	57 g	2.01 oz
⅓ cup	76 g	2.68 oz
½ cup	113 g	3.99 oz
1 cup	227 g	8.00 oz

All-Purpose Flour and Confectioners' Sugar

Cups	Grams	Ounces
⅛ cup	16 g	0.563 oz
¼ cup	32 g	1.13 oz
⅓ cup	43 g	1.50 oz
½ cup	64 g	2.25 oz
⅔ cup	85 g	3.00 oz
¾ cup	96 g	3.38 oz
1 cup	128 g	4.50 oz

Granulated Sugar

Cups	Grams	Ounces
2 tbsp.	25 g	0.89 oz
¼ cup	50 g	1.78 oz
⅓ cup	67 g	2.37 oz
½ cup	100 g	3.55 oz
⅔ cup	134 g	4.73 oz
¾ cup	150 g	5.30 oz
1 cup	201 g	7.10 oz

Packed Brown Sugar

Cups	Grams	Ounces
¼ cup	55 g	1.90 oz
⅓ cup	73 g	2.58 oz
½ cup	110 g	3.88 oz
1 cup	220 g	7.75 oz

Index

First published in 2019 by **riva Verlag**, part of Münchner Verlagsgruppe GmbH. This English language edition published in 2020 by **Lotus Publishing**, Apple Tree Cottage, Inlands Road, Nutbourne, Chichester, PO18 8RJ, UK

Important note
This book is intended for information purposes. It is not a substitute for a personal medical consultation and should not be used as such. For medical advice, please consult a qualified doctor. The publisher and the author shall not be liable for any negative effects directly or indirectly associated with the information given in this book.

Editor: Ulrike Reinen
Cover design: Pamela Machleidt
Photos: p. 3, 14, 15, 35, 247: Christoph Wieboldt
Cover illustrations and all other images on the inside pages: Bianca Zapatka
Layout: Katja Muggli, Medlar Publishing Solutions Pvt Ltd., India
Translation: Surrey Translation Bureau
Printing: Great Britain by Bell and Bain Ltd, Glasgow

British Library Cataloguing-in-Publication Data
A CIP record for this book is available from the British Library.
ISBN 978-1-913088-13-2

You can find more information on the publisher at:

lotuspublishing.co.uk